Early Planning Utopias

Early Planning Utopias

A Feminist Critique

Dorina Pojani, Cathy Keys, and Rory Little

ANTHEM PRESS

Anthem Press
An imprint of Wimbledon Publishing Company
www.anthempress.com

This edition first published in UK and USA 2025
by ANTHEM PRESS
75–76 Blackfriars Road, London SE1 8HA, UK
or PO Box 9779, London SW19 7ZG, UK
and
244 Madison Ave #116, New York, NY 10016, USA

© 2025 Dorina Pojani, Cathy Keys, Rory Little

The author asserts the moral right to be identified as the author of this work.

All rights reserved. Without limiting the rights under copyright reserved above, no part of this publication may be reproduced, stored or introduced into a retrieval system, or transmitted, in any form or by any means (electronic, mechanical, photocopying, recording or otherwise), without the prior written permission of both the copyright owner and the above publisher of this book.

British Library Cataloguing-in-Publication Data
A catalogue record for this book is available from the British Library.

Library of Congress Cataloging-in-Publication Data: 2025931861
A catalog record for this book has been requested.

ISBN-13: 978-1-83999-452-4 (Pbk)
ISBN-10: 1-83999-452-5 (Pbk)

Cover Credit: Wikimedia commons

This title is also available as an e-book.

To all the women pioneers in planning

CONTENTS

Figures ix
About the Authors xi
Acknowledgements xiii

Introduction 1
  Background 3
  Types of Feminism 6
  Selection Criteria 7

Analysis 9
  The Utopian Visionaries 9
    Arturo Soria y Mata's Ciudad Lineal 9
    Ebenezer Howard's Garden City 12
    Frank Lloyd Wright's Broadacre City 15
    Tony Garnier's Cité Industrielle 18
    Bruno Taut's Stadtkrone 20
    Le Corbusier's Cité Radieuse 23
    Antonio Sant'Elia's Città Nuova 26
    Nikolay Milyutin's Sotsgorod 29
  The Rational Functionalists 32
    Titus Salt's and George Pullman's model mill towns 32
    Georges-Eugène Haussmann and the transformation of Paris 36
    Ildefons Cerdà and Barcelona's Eixample plan 40
    Otto Wagner's Die Grossstadt and Vienna's masterplan 44
    Josef Stübben's struggle to balance tradition and modernity 47
    Daniel Burnham's plan of Chicago and the City Beautiful 50
    Patrick Geddes and the advent of biological ideas in planning 53
    John Nolen's merging of nature and urbanism 54
    Patrick Abercrombie's professionalised planning process 57
  The Romantic Archaists 59
    Frederick Law Olmsted's urban parks and garden suburbs 60

Camillo Sitte and city planning as an artistic endeavour	62
Raymond Unwin and the return to picturesque village life	65
Synthesis	67
Central Themes in Masculine Early Utopias	67
Women's Different Planning Preoccupations	71
Conclusion	77
References	79
Notes	87

FIGURES

1	Plan of Ciudad Lineal	10
2	Section of the main street	11
3	Garden City plan section	14
4	Broadacre City sketch	16
5	Aerial view of the centre of Cité Industrielle	18
6	Stadtkrone's aerial view	21
7	Model of the Plan Voisin for Paris, based on the Cité Radieuse principles	24
8	Multi-family building	28
9	Linear city plan for an auto plant	30
10	Aerial view of Saltaire	33
11	Map of Pullman	35
12	Plan, profile, and urban furniture of Avenue de l'Impératrice (now Avenue Foch)	37
13	Aerial view of Avenue des Champs-Élysées and other newly created avenues and boulevards	38
14	Photograph of public works around the Trocadéro	39
15	Enlargement map of Barcelona	42
16	Study for a subway stop entrance	45
17	Street details in Stübben's book	47
18	Proposed design for Chicago, view looking north from Washington Street	52

19	Valley section	54
20	Perspective sketch of the San Diego bayfront, showing the Paseo connecting the bay with the city park	56
21	Road widening project in Liverpool	58
22	Riverside layout, as it appeared in 1950	61
23	Typical illustration in Sitte's book	64
24	Plan for Letchworth	66
25	Austin's designs for kitchenless houses and meal delivery systems	74

ABOUT THE AUTHORS

Dorina Pojani is an associate professor of urban planning at The University of Queensland, Australia, where she has taught planning theory and history. She is the author of 'Trophy Cities: A Feminist Perspective on New Capitals' (Edward Elgar, 2021).

Cathy Keys is a senior lecturer of architectural design at The University of Queensland, Australia, where she has taught architectural design and history. Her research is dedicated to exploring the social and cultural properties of architectural space.

Rory Little is an urban planner and recent graduate of The University of Queensland, Australia. In 2023, he received the Best Undergraduate Submission Award from the UQ Organisation of Planning Students.

ACKNOWLEDGEMENTS

The authors express their gratitude to the School of Architecture, Design and Planning at the University of Queensland, Australia, for providing a research grant which supported this book project. We extend our thanks to the editorial team at Anthem Press for their guidance from inception to publication, to the anonymous peer reviewers for their trust and encouragement, and to our families for their unwavering support.

INTRODUCTION

There is little doubt that urban planning has failed women (Pojani et al. 2018). A series of feminist planners, architects, and human geographers have elucidated the ways in which contemporary cities favour the male gender. Recent books on this topic include *What If Women Designed the City* (East 2024), *She City* (Kalms 2024), *Gendered City* (Bassam 2023), *Trophy Cities* (Pojani 2021), *Feminist City* (Kern 2020), *Engendering Cities* (Sánchez de Madariaga and Neuman 2020), and *Where Are the Women Architects?* (Stratigakos 2016), not to mention a myriad of articles, reports, special issues,[1] and blogs. Similar literature has been produced since the 1970s, as the second wave of the feminist movement gained momentum, and some classic readings have been featured in *Gender and Planning* (Fainstein and Servon 2005).

However, sexism in urban planning was cemented much earlier than second-wave feminism. The urban environments we experience today have been shaped by long-standing systems of gender inequality. In fact, patriarchy has accompanied human civilisation all along, and as such, it has likely affected city planning since antiquity. But during the so-called Second Industrial Revolution[2] – which stretches from the mid- to late 1800s, through the interwar period – patriarchal regimes fused with industrial capitalism to produce a particularly pernicious version of urbanism.

The patriarchy is defined as a social system in which men hold primary power and dominance, systematically oppressing and marginalising women and feminised "others." Meanwhile, industrial capitalism is an economic system where private individuals or corporations own and control the means of production and distribution of goods, driven by the goal of profit. This system became widespread throughout the North Atlantic during the Second Industrial Revolution. It was characterised by large-scale industrial production, technological innovation, and the accumulation of capital through investments and market competition.[3]

Planning, as a profession, was created in the context of patriarchal industrial capitalism. Industrialisation brought about severe urban problems, which are well documented in texts and photographs from that era.[4] By most accounts, the industrial cities of Europe and North America were filthy. Roads were unpaved, undrained, and congested, whereas much of the housing stock was rundown, overcrowded, and poorly lit and ventilated. Homelessness was common. Factories crept up everywhere, their smokestacks polluting the air and their wastage spoiling the water. Workers were undernourished and sickly, and infant mortality was high (Clark and Howard 2003; Smith 2006; Watson 2019).

Concern about these conditions, combined with the looming prospect of civil unrest, prompted efforts at social reforms which gradually evolved into spatial planning standards and models. However, workers' welfare was not the only, nor even the primary, preoccupation of early planners. Cities needed to maximise efficiency and facilitate the movement of labour, goods, and capital to meet the demands of emerging industries. In addition, early planning was heavily influenced by land values and the interests of real estate investors.

In this book, we discuss and critique the work of 20 male planning luminaries who proposed urban models, interventions, and approaches on both sides of the North Atlantic during the Second Industrial Revolution. Our analytical lens is a feminist one. We argue that these early visions and ideas, which purported to be emancipatory and even utopian, set North Atlantic cities on an inexorable masculinist path (Hooper 1998).

As we experience a fourth wave of feminism, the time is ripe to revisit the preconceptions that underpinned early efforts at envisioning new cities or improving existing cities. Indeed, doing so is necessary if we wish to extricate the profession from the patriarchy. While it may be confronting, our analysis is also nuanced. We recognise that early planners were well intentioned, and their designs, while patriarchal, also have essential features which are not alienating or oppressive – in fact, many were superior to the post–World War II designs that followed (Markus 2003).

Before proceeding to the core of the book, we take a cursory look at the existing literature on utopian cities and settlements, and briefly discuss contemporary feminist thought, particularly as it relates to urban planning. We also lay out the selection criteria for the case studies we cover. While we train our lens on male planners and theorists, later in the book we discuss the work of several female activists and reformers from the Second Industrial Revolution era. As we shall see, many of them strove to create better built environments for women but rarely envisioned full-blown urban utopias or wrote lengthy treatises about planning issues.

Background

This book is certainly not the first to tackle utopian cities and settlements. The harbinger of this genre[5] is probably John Humphrey Noyes's book *History of American Socialisms* (2019[1870]). Noyes was the founder of the Oneida Community, a perfectionist religious society in New York State, dedicated to communitarian living and sharing, which lasted for about three decades. The book was written before the community's dissolution, at a time when most other socialist experiments in America had already failed. Noyes provided a comprehensive survey of these past experiments, examining their histories, founders, housing arrangements, daily life, and finally their downfalls, in order to provide lessons for future utopian socialist endeavours. The book focused on two groups of experiments: those related to Owenism and those related to Fourierism (see notes 8 and 9) – but also considered other communities which straddle these two movements.

Half a century later, another book in the genre appeared: *The Story of Utopias* by Lewis Mumford (1922), which was broader in scope. An American historian and social critic, Mumford made a substantial contribution to urban planning discourse in the twentieth century. In this early work, he described in minute detail utopian models ranging from Plato's Republic to H. G. Wells's Modern Utopia, examining their socio-philosophical underpinnings.

Another half-century passed before the next substantial book on urban utopias appeared. In 1976, Dolores Hayden published *Seven American Utopias: The Architecture of Communitarian Socialism, 1790–1975*, reprising the theme of collectivist settlements in the United States. She covered seven historical case studies – four religious and three non-sectarian – and explored how their architecture and building processes reflected their respective ideologies and styles of social organisation. Unlike Noyes and Mumford, Hayden was quite interested in *feminist* utopias. Throughout the book, she commented, albeit briefly, on the roles of women. Alice Constance Austin's design of the community of Llano del Rio (see page 74) featured as a prominent example.

In 1982 Hayden (1982) followed up with *The Grand Domestic Revolution: A History of Feminist Designs for American Homes, Neighbourhoods, and Cities*. This later work exhaustively analysed the wider history of the American feminist movement from the mid-nineteenth century to the early twentieth century in an effort to rediscover the lost tradition of material feminism.[6] Hayden's book was also a tribute to some of the leaders of this movement – Melusina Fay Peirce, Charlotte Perkins Gilman, and Marie Stevens Howland. Not only were these women interested in politics and economics but also in spatial and practical matters; they pioneered concepts such as cooperative housekeeping and kitchenless houses (see page 71).

The lead author of the next book in the genre, *Utopia on Trial: Vision and Reality in Planned Housing* (1985), was also a woman, Alice Coleman (Coleman et al. 1985). An influential British geographer, she made no claim of adopting a feminist perspective. Her book only touched upon the concept of utopia in its opening pages to note that post-war planned housing estates in Britain were initially envisioned as Modernist utopian creations. Then, using the analogy of a legal trial, Coleman and her colleagues proceeded to provide statistical evidence of the failures and "social malaises" evident in housing estates by the 1970s. They attributed these problems – which physically manifested as litter, graffiti, vandalism, and excrement – to ill-fitting Modernist design features.

Dennis Hardy's book *Utopian England: Community Experiments 1900–1945* (2012) focused on the earlier part of the twentieth century. Hardy showed that utopian thought and practice were widespread in the Victorian era, paving the way for popular planning concepts that followed, such as the Garden City. In evaluating and comparing his case studies, Hardy recognised that most utopian communities were male-dominated and poorly served the interests of women.

Ruth Eaton's (2002) book *Ideal Cities: Utopianism and the (un)built Environment* was broader in scope. It may be considered as an update and expansion of Helen Rosenau's long essay "The Ideal City in its Architectural Evolution," which was published in 1959. Eaton reviewed two millennia of Western efforts to conceive the perfect city and society. This exploration extended beyond architecture and urban planning, encompassing art, literature, philosophy, and politics. The book covered movements and figures ranging from Filarete to the European Situationists. However, Eaton's portrayal of ideal cities largely existed within the realm of abstract ideas, some achieved and some failed, and her analysis was not necessarily from a feminist perspective.

Embodied Utopias: Gender, Social Change and the Modern Metropolis, edited by Amy Bingaman, Lise Sanders, Rebecca Zorach (2002) made up for the missing feminist perspective. Uniquely, it drew together themes of urban space, gender, body, and utopia. The contributing authors sought to redefine the concept of utopia, moving away from the traditional, male-dominated notion of an ideal society towards a dynamic process characterised by continual negotiation, confrontation, resistance, and creation. This revised understanding framed utopia as an ongoing journey rather than a fixed destination. The topics traversed diverse realms, moving from Gilded Age Washington, D.C., to socialist Hanoi to cyberspace. However, much of the book focused on interior architecture and domestic spaces rather than the urban scale.

The most recent addition to this genre is Kristen Ghodsee's (2023) *Everyday Utopia: What 2,000 Years of Wild Experiments Can Teach Us About the Good Life*. This book reviews the history of utopian social experiments to extract and foreground ways of improving various facets of contemporary life. For example, one chapter discusses cohabitation with nonconsanguineous others, linking this to the growth of Danish-style co-housing arrangements. Ghodsee's perspective is clearly feminist: she often stops to examine gender roles and points to utopias that sought to improve women's lives. She also notes the proto-feminist attitudes of idealists like Plato. Nonetheless, as an ethnographer, Ghodsee focuses on the private sphere rather than the physical aspects that interest urban planners the most.

Notably, only a few of these books delve specifically into the concept of 'feminist utopias'. There is a good reason behind this absence: feminist utopias have primarily existed within the realm of literature rather than as a blueprint for urban planning.[7] Books by Barr and Smith (1983), Kessler (1984), and Bartowski (1989), which present and critique feminist utopias from the nineteenth century onwards, have played a crucial role in reshaping academia's perception of tradition in utopian fiction. Prior to the second wave of the feminist movement, this tradition was largely defined through a male-centric lens. In reality, a number of feminist utopias were conceived within the timeframe covered by our study (the Second Industrial Revolution), reflecting a mounting interest in women's issues, as well as a growing pool of female writers and readers of fiction.

Some writers yearned for separatist, all-female communities, whereas others attempted to define non-sexist communities that catered to men and women equally (Mellor 1982). Despite these divergences, there are also many continuities in this literature. Writers pondered similar issues affecting women, such as the fear of rape or assault, the heavy toil of housework and childrearing, children's illegitimacy, highly gendered labour markets, sex-linked traits and appearance, and claustrophobic nuclear families run by male patriarchs (Pearson 1977). The recurring themes in feminist utopian visions are: education as a means to liberation and empowerment; an optimistic view of humans as capable of change and improvement; gradual rather than revolutionary change; non-hierarchical, quasi-anarchic governance; respect for non-human nature; and pragmatism as opposed to spirituality (Johns 2010).

Evidently, women felt deeply alienated, oppressed, and constrained by patriarchal society. Having little political clout to change reality, they envisioned fantastical alternatives in which they could realise their potential. These alternative societies have typically been nimble and process-oriented, rather than ideal 'end states'. In contrast, the utopian visions of male writers have more often depicted "static perfection – societies so ideal that they have nowhere to go, rely on rigid hierarchies and use coercion to maintain their perfect order" (Johns 2010: 174). These are clearly objectionable societies in which women fare poorly. However, process-oriented, "reproductive" utopias, which lack visualisations or detailed descriptions of outcomes in terms of built environment, have limited relevance for urban planners.

Types of Feminism

At its core, feminism is the advocacy for women's rights and the equality of the sexes. The feminist movement seeks to combat misogyny, which positions women as inferior to men. As a progressive force aiming to emancipate society, fight prejudice, challenge inherited practices, and shape future actions, feminism can be viewed as an offshoot of the ever-evolving project of humanism (Johnson 2015). Since its first wave at the turn of the twentieth century, the movement has developed many strands, some of which conflict with one another. Two broad camps have formed: 'essentialists', who believe that differences between men and women have biological roots, and 'environmentalists', who regard gender as a cultural construct. However, there are major schisms within these camps.

Liberal feminism, for example, focuses on achieving gender equality through legal reforms, education, and workplace opportunities, emphasising individual rights and advancement within existing structures. In contrast, *Marxist feminists* view the capitalistic workplace as a key enabler of women's oppression. They argue that simply integrating women into the workforce does not solve the underlying exploitation of labour or unpaid domestic work. *Ecofeminists* add that patriarchy is also intertwined with environmental destruction and that true liberation requires dismantling exploitative systems rather than allowing women to take from nature as much as men.

Other debates exist between *radical feminists*, who see gender and heterosexual relationships as tools of oppression that must be abolished, and *intersectional feminists*, who highlight the need to address race, class, and other axes of identity alongside gender. *Post-colonial feminism* challenges North Atlantic narratives that assume a universal experience of womanhood, instead emphasising how imperialism, race, and culture have shaped gender oppression differently across the world. Drawing from traditions of Black activism and spirituality, *womanism* emphasises collective healing, community uplift, and intergenerational solidarity. Womanists embrace family and motherhood as sources of strength.

Our analysis is grounded in the tenets of *social-anarcha-feminism* (see Bottici 2022), a strand that focuses on the broader project of dismantling all hierarchical and oppressive structures in society, including the state, the capitalist system, and the patriarchy. Social anarcha-feminists support consensus-based, horizontal forms of organisation, and believe in direct action, mutual aid, and voluntary cooperation. This movement is closely aligned with ecofeminism, which also supports the notion that life in nature is sustained by means of cooperation, reciprocal care, and love (Mies and Shiva 2014).

Viewed through this lens, urban planning and governance systems – current and historical – are symbolically gendered by a conception of leadership as hierarchical and domineering. The very idea of concentrating decision-making power in the hands of a small elite of designers, bureaucrats, and politicians rather than distributing it to the masses is patriarchal in character. In contrast, feminist ethics emphasise values grounded in relationships and compassion for humans and non-human beings (Hendler 2005).

We envision a social-anarcha-feminist city as a polity founded on what are commonly regarded as "female" values of "caretaking, nurturing, and mothering" (Goettner-Abendroth 2010: 2). This approach turns gender essentialism on its head. Rather than avoiding or rejecting stereotypical feminine values, planners are encouraged to embrace and harness them as guiding principles. These values are redefined and applied in ways that transcend traditional gender boundaries, promoting inclusivity and empathy in urban spaces.

The following 10 principles, inspired by Markus (2003), provide a starting point for a social anarcha-feminist approach to city-making: (1) respect for, rather than exploitation of, nature; (2) scepticism about the promised benefits of technology; (3) integration of local and global space rather than worldwide homogenisation; (4) fragmentary rather than monolithic build forms; (5) freedom for creativity and spontaneous development rather than rigid rules and prohibitions; (6) human scale to regions, cities, neighbourhoods, and buildings; (7) freedom to use public space or retreat to private space, whether gender-mixed or women-only; (8) a range of unprescribed living, dwelling, and working patterns and spaces; (9) health, safety, and well-being for humans and non-human species; and (10) more space for reproduction and care rather than for production and growth.

Selection Criteria

A project such as this, aiming to cover nearly one hundred years of planning history on both sides of the North Atlantic, necessitates clear boundaries. The 20 early planners discussed and critiqued in this book were selected based on a set of pre-defined criteria, which we spell out below.

Our timeline (mid-1800s through the interwar period) loosely coincides with the Second Industrial Revolution. A focus on ideas and plans that appeared during this time excludes eighteenth-century utopian thinkers such as Charles Fourier[8] or Robert Owen,[9] whose contributions to planning theory are nonetheless important. We cover exclusively Europe and North America because this is where modern planning thought gelled. However, ideas from this region spread to the rest of the world either via coercion (in the context of colonisation) or through voluntary exchanges. For example, Georges-Eugène Haussmann's approach in Paris influenced Tehran's planning during Reza Shah Pahlavi reign (Mehan 2017), as well as Tokyo's reconstruction plan after the 1923 Great Kantō earthquake (Hein 2010), while Arturo Soria y Mata's ideas for Madrid were taken to Santiago, Chile (Collins 1959a).

We selected authors whose written work is available in English (either in the original or in translation).[10] This excluded several key figures such as Reinhard Baumeister,[11] Charles Buls,[12] Hendrik Petrus Berlage,[13] and Eugène Alfred Hénard,[14] whose work is only available in their native languages. In addition, we sought to include people who devoted their time to both planning practice and theory. This left out leading theorists like Lewis Mumford[15] or practitioners like Robert Moses.[16] All the authors we included were engaged in spatial planning. Those who, in their writings, targeted primarily the economic, legal, and technical aspects of planning and construction, such as Walter Moody,[17] Frederick Howe,[18] Edward Bassett,[19] Rexford Tugwell,[20] and George Ford,[21] were omitted from our list;[22] so was Benjamin Ward Richardson, a doctor and public health specialist.[23] Authors of utopian fiction, such as Edward Bellamy,[24] were also excluded.

Many planners and theorists were active in the United States during our timeline; in the interest of geographical balance, we only included the most prominent ones. Lesser-known figures such as Charles Mulford Robinson,[25] Nelson Peter Lewis,[26] and Werner Hegemann[27] were left out. We also excluded urban models that were developed for marketing purposes – for example, Futurama,[28] sponsored by General Motors, a company with an explicit commercial interest in promoting car ownership and driving.

ANALYSIS

This analysis is structured into three parts. The first part discusses eight 'utopian visionaries' who proposed fully developed urban utopias, ranging from the Linear City in Spain to the Socialist City in the Soviet Union. Next is a set of authors who sought ways to improve existing cities. These are divided into 'rational functionalists' (15 authors) and 'romantic archaists' (three authors) – after Schorske's (1981) terminology with reference to *fin-de-siècle* Vienna and its ideologically and emotionally charged struggle between modernism and anti-modernism (Cortjaens 2011). Within each part, authors are listed chronologically by birth date.

The Utopian Visionaries

These planners sought to visualise the ideal – either retrospective or futuristic – rather than perpetuate the quotidian.

Arturo Soria y Mata's Ciudad Lineal

Arturo Soria y Mata (1844–1920), trained as an engineer in Madrid, was a capitalistic entrepreneur and inventor. He also held posts in public administration in Spain and its colonies – despite being a radical republican who was often at odds with Spanish monarchists. As an outspoken advocate of technological innovation, particularly in the field of transport, he insisted that circulation is the key organising factor of the modern city (Collins 1959a,b). As a social critic, he was quite concerned by the unsanitary housing conditions of Madrid workers, which he thought led to moral decay:

> The unlucky worker, condemned to live in a narrow, unventilated, dirty, and overcrowded room cannot enjoy the few spare moments of family life that he has. It is hardly surprising that he leaves the house and ends up in the tavern, to later land in jail […] The worker's wife protests with a simple but very eloquent act. She will place a flower pot with some bright geraniums on her attic window ledge […] With time,

these flowers will kindle the hope for a true urban life and the desire to harmonize the sweetness of country life with the undeniable advantages of the city. (Soria y Mata 1892[2004])

This is the only mention of gender in relation to urban space. Interestingly, this passage suggests that men are prone to succumbing to vices, whereas women, even working-class women, are a civilising force in a coarse urban environment.

Like Haussmann in Paris (see page 36), Soria believed that urban renewal was long overdue in Madrid, and this involved expropriating and clearing large swaths of land (Soria y Mata 1892[2004]). He was the first to propose, in 1892, a Linear City model as a counterpoint to the wanton growth of concentric cities (Figure 1). His city was developed along a wide boulevard of indefinite length; its width, in contrast, was limited to a 500-metre band (Figure 2). Cross streets were placed every 300 metres, creating large residential blocks. Buildings had modest heights and were separated by dense vegetation. Departing from the Mediterranean tradition of multi-family living, the Linear City provided each resident with their own house and garden – presumably to restore dignity, health, and individuality. The minimum lot size was 1/10th acre. Larger homes faced the main thoroughfares, while smaller housing faced interior streets. This arrangement did not challenge the class system but enabled close proximity between rich and poor. The urban plan incorporated spaces for workshops, stores, markets, churches, and other amenities. Agricultural production was encouraged beyond the urbanised spine (Boileau 1959).

Like other urban utopias, Soria's Linear City was about conquering space. It proposed to do so in horizontal strips as opposed to Le Corbusier's

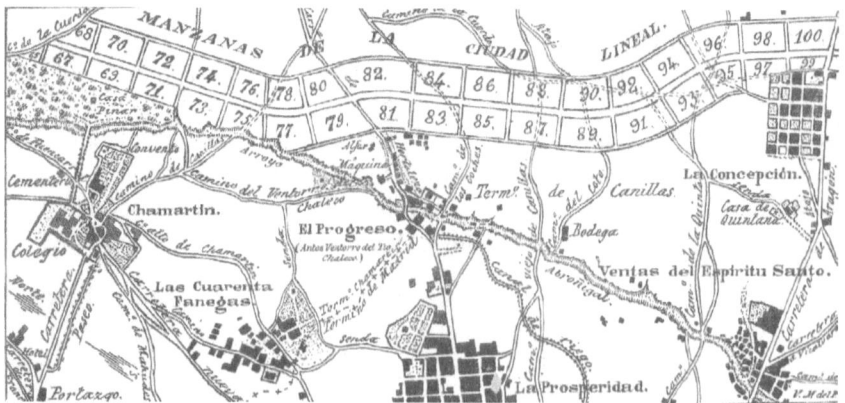

Figure 1 Plan of Ciudad Lineal. Source: Wikimedia Commons. Image in the public domain.

Figure 2 Section of the main street. Source: Wikimedia Commons. Image in the public domain.

verticality in the Radiant City or Howard's regional pointillism of Garden Cities (see pages 12 and 23) (Fraser 2019). Soria anticipated three different uses of a Linear City: (1) to form suburban extensions; (2) to physically connect existing cities across the world ("Cadiz and Saint Petersburg, or Peking and Brussels"); and (3) to colonise "leftover" lands (Collins 1959). As such, the model encapsulated a political ideology: stopping or reversing rural-urban migration trends by merging city and village environments. Soria's motto was to "ruralize urban life, urbanize the countryside" (Soria y Mata 1892[2004]).

To turn his vision into a reality, Soria established a streetcar company and a construction company. He also founded a planning journal called Ciudad Lineal (the first of its kind in Spain), which for decades would tirelessly promote Soria's ideas, as well as the pilot linear suburb (Ciudad Lineal) that was eventually built along a short tram stretch on the outskirts of Madrid. By the late 1920s, this suburb had about 2,500 dwellings (Boileau 1959). By the 1950s, both the tramline and the Ciudad Lineal were taken over by the City of Madrid, which had already grown to nearly two million inhabitants.

In hindsight, some commentaries have praised Soria's Linear City for being "undetermined" – as opposed to the "limited and provincial" Garden City proposed by Howard (see page 12) (Frampton 1992). However, the two models are similar in their low-density housing and insulating zones of vegetation. A critique of the linear model is its lack of a central function, such as business or administration, which is a city's raison d'être, according to Modernist planners (Doxiadis 1967). In fact, early accounts indicated that Soria paid little attention to the systematic provision of shops, forcing residents to travel to nearby villages for their daily shopping (Boileau 1959).

Other commentators have criticised Soria's concept for preserving the status quo in urban class relationships (Fraser 2019). In reality, the Madrid experiment embodied both financial interests and an altruistic mission of enhancing the quality of life for the poor. It aimed to redistribute land and eliminate the tyranny and parasitism of landlordship. The design sought to ensure that property prices declined gradually from the main thoroughfare to parallel streets, avoiding the abrupt drops of concentric cities. Soria prioritised affordable workers' housing, constructing homes for as little as $800. However, parts of the Ciudad Lineal functioned as a summer retreat for wealthy *madrileños* (Collins 1959).

Besides the plan, Soria himself has been critiqued as an exemplification of "the archetypal, obsessive figure of the nineteenth century modern urban planner" (Fraser 2019). His fixation with the straight line – lauded as the most economic, progressive, moral, and democratic shape – is evident in his extensive writings on the Linear City project, as well as his treatise on geometry (*Origen Poliédrico De Las Especies*). (Oddly, in the latter, he classifies various polyhedral forms as having strictly male or female sex characteristics, which suggests a deeply essentialist view of gender.)

While Soria appears dogmatic in his theoretical musings, he showed some flexibility in his practice. For example, the full tram line he envisioned was a radial one, connecting suburbs while bypassing the city centre. This was an innovation that was later adopted in many Spanish cities. Madrid's Ciudad Lineal was meant to be developed along both sides of this tram line. Had it been realised in its entirety, the project would have been in the shape of a horseshoe circling Madrid – rather than the perfectly straight line of the conceptual model (Boileau 1959; Doxiadis 1967).

Despite its limited execution, the Linear City model and plan had a wide impact on international planning culture. For example, Soviet planners like Nikolay Milyutin toyed with the idea of linear communities in the 1930s (see page 29). The finger-like extensions of Northern European cities such as Copenhagen and Amsterdam are also fashioned after the linear city concept and work quite well in terms of accessibility. In the United States, on the other hand, the Linear City translated into 'ribbon' or 'strip' development along suburban "stroads," whose blight was already evident in the 1950s (Collins 1959).[1] Now, veritable megalopolises have formed across the continents – for example, along the American northeastern coast or the Australian east coast. These are increasingly difficult to manage due to their colossal size and interconnected nature.

Ebenezer Howard's Garden City

Ebenezer Howard (1850–1928) was an English public servant who began to develop his ideas about an alternative type of city during the 1870s while working in Chicago and coming across architect and urban planner Daniel Burnham (see page 50). Upon his return to England, he was also exposed to social reformers who lamented the loss of a rural, healthy, and dignified lifestyle in English industrial cities. Similarly, in his writings, Howard decried "crowded, ill-vented, unplanned, unwieldy, unhealthy cities – ulcers on the very face of our beautiful island" (Howard 1902). According to Howard, the solution lay in building a network of small, self-contained, and self-sufficient 'Garden Cities' on greenfield sites, with plenty of access to parks, surrounded by agricultural land, and linked by train lines (Clark and Howard 2003). He publicised this idea in his 1902 book *Garden Cities of Tomorrow*.

The book appealed to men who saw the city as the site of growing class conflict. On the left of the political spectrum were calls for more municipal responsibility or even municipal socialism. On the right side were the private property defenders and the 'small government' advocates (Flanagan 2018). A maverick alpha male, Howard sought to reconcile the two ideological sides – as well as urban and rural lifestyles – by promoting a third way: small-scale communitarianism. Like other men of his time, Howard believed that a reorganisation of the physical environments of cities could trigger social change (Greed 1994).

He proposed that the land for each Garden City be purchased by a group of trustees who would hold it in trust for the residents. Residents and businesses would not own the land outright but would lease it from the community. Any profits generated from the lease of land were to be reinvested back into the community. This was intended to prevent speculative increases in land values and to ensure that the benefits of any increase in land value would accrue to the community. In crowded industrial cities, lower-income men were trapped in "a vicious circle of paying rents and rates to large landowners," but in Garden Cities, they could once again be masters of their homes (Flanagan 2018: 93). In a sense, these schemes aimed to help lower-income men restore their lost sense of masculinity.

Physically, Howard's Garden City could only support 30,000–32,000 people. The plan shape was concentric: radiating from a green centre, six broad boulevards created six city districts (Figure 3). Commercial and civic functions were built in the next ring out and then encircled by another large public park. Housing formed the next ring out, bounded by a radial Grand Avenue, and accompanied by schools and gardens. Homes were on individual lots, allowing residents to produce their own food. The outer ring held industrial workplaces, such as factories, dairies, warehouses, and markets. A railway line was also placed on the outer ring. Finally, an agricultural belt encircled the city, restricting its growth (Howard 1902). The distances between homes, workplaces, and fields were quite small. Howard envisaged that, in a Garden City, people would travel on foot or by public transport and bicycle. The latter was a novelty at the time and quite popular among liberal women (Greed 1994).

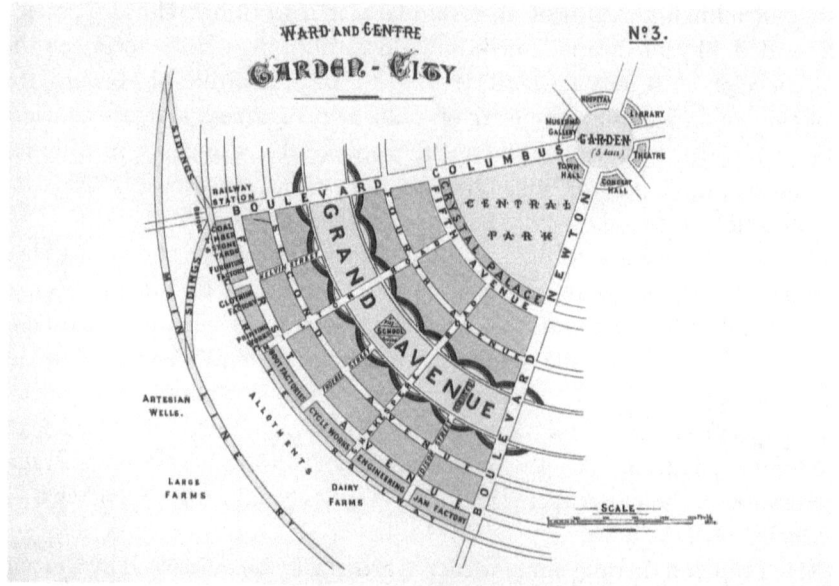

Figure 3 Garden City plan section. Source: Wikimedia Commons. Image in the public domain.

While these physical and economic aspects were innovative, the Garden City was undergirded by gender-based ideas about the public and private spheres. To Howard, men and women were complementary (but not equal), just as city and country were. This meant that residents' roles and spaces in the Garden City were clearly divided by gender. The domestic and working realms were carefully separated. While men built the Garden City, women managed the domestic setting (Meller 1990) and civilized society through their domesticating practices (Flanagan 2018: 94–95). Each neighbourhood was clearly defined, and each home, containing a nuclear family, was separated from its neighbours by a garden. There was no loitering on the streets, no idle chat in doorways, and no ground-floor shops staffed by women (Flanagan 2018). Overall, as Jacobs (1961: 27,28) has noted, Howard's Garden City concept was paternalistic:

> His aim was the creation of self-sufficient small towns, really very nice small towns if you were docile and had no plans of your own and did not mind spending your time among others with no plans of their own [...]. For Howard was envisioning not simply a physical environment and social life, but a paternalistic political and economical society.

Howard's Garden City did not remain only a utopian ideal. His book inspired the creation of a Garden City Association, and three practical experiments were undertaken in England before World War II: Welwyn, Wythenshawe, and Letchworth. The latter was designed by Raymond Unwin (see page 65). English writer and social critic H. G. Wells panned these Garden City plans for having "no provision directed towards liberating women from their role as defined by traditional interpretations of the Two Spheres" (cited in Meller 1990: 84–85). In fairness, Howard did endorse feminist ideas such as cooperative housekeeping and shared centralised kitchen facilities, which were conceived by some of the leading female reformers of that era, including Melusina Fay Peirce, Marie Stevens Case Howland, and Charlotte Perkins Gilman (see page 71). Possibly, he did so because, like many middle-class men, he wished to reduce the need for domestic servants rather than undo male–female dichotomies (Greed 1994).

Regardless of Howard's motivations, one of Letchworth's districts contained 32 kitchenless apartments in which the tenants used common kitchens and shared domestic work based on cooperative housekeeping principles. Howard built a second cooperative housekeeping project at Letchworth and a third one at Welwyn. These projects demonstrated awareness by Howard and his collaborating planners of the housing needs of "unconventional" groups such as single women, older adults, widowed people, childless couples, and two-worker households. However, the cooperative housekeeping projects did not generate mass demand for similar facilities (Hayden 1982). In contrast, the low-density housing model of Garden Cities inspired myriad faceless suburbs across the North Atlantic.

Frank Lloyd Wright's Broadacre City

Frank Lloyd Wright (1867–1959) was an American architect and designer who developed a unique style of architecture based on principles from the Arts and Crafts movement. Designing numerous structures and houses in what became known as the Prairie Style around Chicago, he sought to create architecture that highlighted nature and simplicity. Wright became increasingly critical of the impacts of densely populated and highly centralised cities on 'men', noting:

> Men of genius, productive when unsuccessful, "succeed," become vicarious, and except those whose metier is the crowd, these men, who should be human salvage, sink in the city to produce, but create no more. Impotent. (Wright 1932: 4)

Convinced by the late 1920s that technical developments in transport and communication had made the centralised American city redundant, Wright developed an alternative model (Figure 4). With the publication of *The Disappearing City* in 1932, he proposed a highly planned settlement promoting low-density housing, industrial estates, and local markets spread over the countryside (Wright 1932; Dougherty 1981). This type of design reflected a process of commercially driven suburban expansion that was already under way in American cities.

Unlike some of his contemporaries in Europe, Wright saw home and land ownership as a precondition for democracy. In his mind, individual agency and freedom could only be supported if distinctions between rural and urban living were removed by building single-family houses on agricultural land, connected to each other and to workplaces by a network of wide roads (Watson 2019). The houses would be occupied by conventional nuclear families headed by a male breadwinner (Fishman 1982). While the plan was socially conservative, Wright waxed lyrical about its physical planning "advances":

> Imagine spacious landscaped highways [...] Giant roads, themselves great architecture, pass public service stations, no longer eyesores, expanded to include all kinds of service and comfort. They unite and

Figure 4 Broadacre City sketch. Source: Kjell Olsen. Licence: CC BY-SA 2.0.

separate – separate and unite the series of diversified units, the farm units, the factory units, the roadside markets, the garden schools, the dwelling places (each on its acre of individually adorned and cultivated ground), the places for pleasure and leisure. [...] I see his buildings modern, sanitary, living conveniences, his wherever he is or wants to be, and as economically as his motor car is his – by a few hours' devotion to machinery. I see the factory too, divided and operated in humane proportions not far away from him in the country; the time spent in any ceaseless to and fro from the office, senseless and waste time that may be well spent in the new individual centralization – the only one that is a real necessity, or a great luxury or a great human asset – his diversified modern Home. I see that home not so far away from the diversified farm units but that may bring him, at the highway wayside markets, as his passes, food, fresh every hour. (Wright 1932: 44,46)

Wright was critical of traffic congestion in existing cities and was convinced that this problem would be eliminated if the existing urban form was diluted beyond recognition. Fascinated by the technological opportunities of the automobile and the airplane, his interpretation of "not so far away" distances between destinations was quite fantastical:

Each citizen of the future will have all forms of production, distribution, self improvement, enjoyment, within a radius of a hundred and fifty miles of his home now easily and speedily available by means of his car or his plane. (Wright 1932: 44)

Clearly, Wright's vision targeted white, middle-class citizens. At the time of his writing, significant inequalities in access to cars, by income and consequently race, existed. Black Americans were segregated into ghettos and lacked the ability to move about and reap the benefits of Wright's pastoral ideal. While the book mentioned factories and farms, the Broadacre City was hardly a place for the working classes. Arguably, it was underpinned by a gendered archetype of a "gentleman of leisure" who spent large swaths of time tending to his garden (Hayden 2004). Wright's houses "created a domestic refuge from both the perceived corrupting influences of the industrial city and the rugged hardship of the rural hinterlands" (Watson 2019: 1008). While the Broadacre City house may have been a sanctuary for men, it was a place of domestic labour for the women stuck at home.

Tony Garnier's Cité Industrielle

Tony Garnier (1869–1948) was a French architect and planner. He is best known for his 'Cité Industrielle', a concept of an ideal industrial city of 35,000 people, drafted between 1901 and 1917 (Figure 5). His plan provides a rich context for feminist critiques. While the plan is meant to be a prototype for an ideal socialist city, it is clearly located in the vicinity of Lyon, Garnier's city of origin. Later versions were informed by the architect's professional experience in Lyon. It is noteworthy that Garnier's philosophy did not change significantly throughout the plan's development (Wiebenson 1960). This continuity is crucial when analysing the feminist implications of the plan.

Garnier's urban plan is impressively detailed, with architectural features, dimensions, and functional zoning laid out meticulously (Wiebenson 1960). This level of detail appears contradictory to Garnier's democratic ideals, suggesting a technocratic aspect to his vision. The industrial city envisioned by Garnier is self-sufficient, with heavy industry as its economic base. The largest employer is a metallurgic factory, presumably employing predominantly men, while a smaller silk manufacturing factory is more likely to hire women. These industrial choices, which lead to gendered employment, are justified as rooted in the natural resources of the area.

However, gender divisions start earlier, during schooling. Garnier's plan emphasises equality of the sexes in primary schools, where boys and girls would study together (Garnier 1989[1917]). However, this equality diminishes in secondary schools, which are designed to cater to the industrial needs of the region, leading to separate classrooms and presumably subjects for boys and girls. The plan includes employment services and sprawling assembly

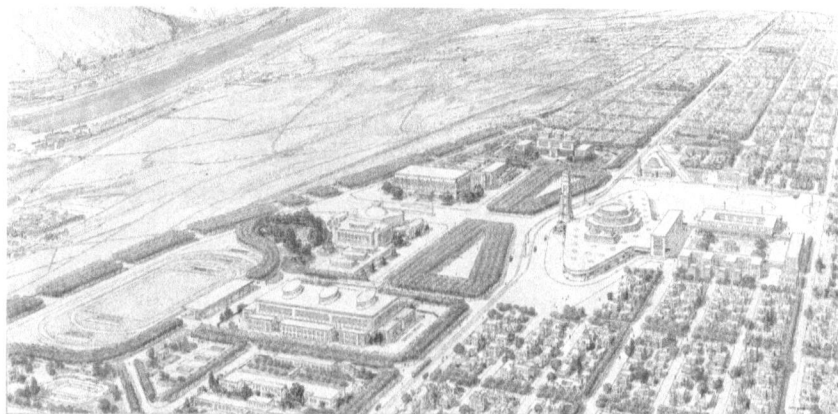

Figure 5 Aerial view of the centre of Cité Industrielle. Source: Lyon MBA. Photo by Alain Basset. Licence CC BY-SA 4.0.

rooms, which are integral to the industrial city's governance structure based on syndicates. This vision aligns with socialist feminism and its tenets of collective decision-making and social support systems. However, it is unclear whether Garnier expected women, as well as men, to use these facilities.

Garnier's concept of segregating functional zones and separating those through green belts is typical of the modern era (Frampton 1992). While his city is relatively small, the drawings suggest its potential to expand into the horizon (Frampton 1992). While the residential neighbourhoods of Garnier's drawings are populated by women socialising with one another in shared green spaces, in reality, single-family zoning can lead to social isolation.

Garnier envisions a society free of courts, police, and jails. He believed that the suppression of capitalism would lead to a society without swindlers, robbers, or murderers (Wiebenson 1960). This aligns with feminist ideals that advocate pacifism and the end of imprisonment. Unsurprisingly, Garnier's city does not include churches; he replaces divine worship with the worship of humans and nature. Like Marxist feminists, Garnier disliked organised religion.

The plan idealises nature and green spaces (Frampton 1992) – although natural resources are also open to exploitation for economic development. For example, a large dam is built on the river while mines in the hinterland provide raw materials for the metallurgic factory. The latter's graphic representation is not romanticised (Wiebenson 1960): instead, industry is shown in all its brutality and inhumanity.

At the same time, Garnier's emphasis on exercise, hygiene, sunlight, and ventilation reflects a concern for the well-being of families, particularly mothers, who often bear the responsibility for their family's health and nutrition. This aligns with feminist ideals centred on care, 'mothering', and well-being. Garnier's emphasis on a horizontal city design is aligned with his use of concrete – a new material at the time.

Garnier's housing designs vary in size and layout, accommodating different types of households. This is unique for that era. However, single-family homes with communal open spaces are a significant feature. Designed to accommodate nuclear families, these homes align with the traditional gender roles of the time, where women were primarily responsible for homemaking and childcare. It is worth noting a few instances where women are portrayed indoors: in both cases, they are carrying or serving food.

Another feminist critique is that the plan's larger houses, such as those designed for the factory's administrative staff, are set in extra-low densities – reflecting social hierarchies. There is no indication that larger houses will accommodate extended families or multiple generations living together, with women sharing caregiving responsibilities. Garnier does include some semi-detached houses or co-housing units with shared covered gardens, concepts that may foster collaboration among residents – men and women – in maintaining the shared space.

Some houses in the plan include private car garages, and some streets depict cars, suggesting the anticipation of widespread car ownership. This feature aligns with the progressive views at that time. However, it is important to consider that, at the period of the plan's creation, women were not widely involved in the workforce, and men were typically the primary drivers of family cars.

While the plan primarily adheres to the gender norms of the early twentieth century, it does display some forward-thinking elements that hint at potential progress in women's roles and opportunities within the home and society. For example, within some housing units, Garnier envisions the incorporation of artist studios or offices – which could serve men or women. This aspect of the plan recognises the potential for flexible, work-from-home situations, which are now commonplace in the post-industrial city.

Bruno Taut's Stadtkrone

Bruno Taut (1880–1938) was a widely acclaimed architect and an early proponent of Expressionism.[2] His career started in Germany before World War I and concluded in exile, as his homeland became increasingly repressive in the interwar period (Whyte 1982). While still in Germany, he served as the chief city planner of Magdeburg and the chief architect of a Berlin association of workers' housing cooperatives. Taut's realised works included exhibition pavilions and residential and industrial projects, with low- and middle-income housing. Also, he engaged in futuristic fantasies, partly out of concern about the artistic insipidness, chaotic growth, and moral decay of the modern European city and partly to occupy his time, as architectural commissions had dried up during the war and in the early Weimar Republic (Whyte 1982). His main urban utopia, titled the City Crown (Die Stadtkrone), was envisioned during the war and published as a booklet in 1919 (Figure 6).

Taut (2009[1919]) described the city as having a circular layout, approximately seven kilometres in diameter. This layout accommodated 300,000 inhabitants initially, with a potential for expansion up to 500,000. The distance from the periphery to the city centre was limited to three kilometres. Residential streets were narrow, while broad thoroughfares accommodated streetcars and car traffic. One section accommodated industries and a train line. Businesses and administration buildings were placed between the train station and the centre. Another section featured a large park seeking to merge

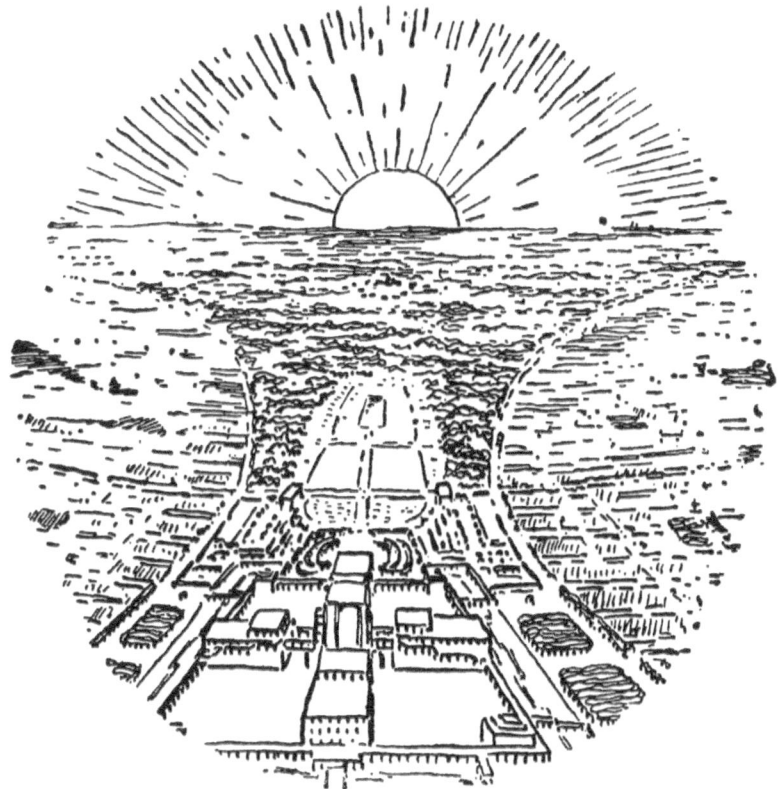

Figure 6 Stadtkrone's aerial view. Source: Wikimedia Commons. Image in the public domain.

the rural and the urban. Houses were low-rise and single-family, with deep gardens.

At the centre lay the 'city crown', on a rectangular area measuring 800 × 500 metres. The crown was strategically placed, tangent to main road arteries radiating wide arcs from its centre. Its base was formed by four large structures accommodating community and leisure activities (theatres, libraries, and the like). These were topped by a tall, dazzling, and functionless glass building. Symbolically, this sacred City Crown served as a magnetic field, fixing the urban space around it. It embodied transcendence, inviting visitors to partake in aesthetic communion. Its transparent and glittery material was a metaphor for higher consciousness and cosmic aspirations for human societies (Miller 2017).

The City Crown representations amalgamate the self-contained Garden City layout and Camillo Sitte's picturesque and coherent vistas (see pages 12 and 62) (Collins and Collins 1965). Like Sitte, Taut quoted Aristotle on the need to create healthy and happy cities. He used examples from pre-modern European, Indian, Chinese, and Ottoman cities to support his view that people tend towards an organic unity in their settlements when left to their own devices, with the skyline accented by a key monument (i.e. "the crown"), typically religious in nature (Akcan 2006). Acknowledging that religion had lost its power as society's moral compass and source of meaning, Taut proposed a non-political socialism as the new faith. In contrast to the class struggles that preoccupied labour unions at the time, this version of socialism was described as "the urge to somehow enhance the well-being of mankind, to achieve salvation for self and others and to feel as one, solidly united with all mankind" (Taut 2009[1919]). The City Crown was designed to reflect this philosophy.

While inspirational and literary, the City Crown text was also riddled with contradictions, like Taut himself. On the one hand, he was a lifelong pacifist and anti-capitalist who claimed to believe in public interest and egalitarianism. However, there was an unresolved tension between individualism and community in his utopian city. While delimited within a circle, the City Crown had no borders and no context. In some passages, Taut clearly assigned a privileged and even sanctified role to the architect (referred to as 'he'), who, as a "pure" creative, was to replace disgraced politicians and antiquated messiahs in guiding the masses towards enlightenment (Colistra 2023; Akcan 2006). This type of activism appears elitist and bourgeois (Whyte 1982).

At one point, Taut even suggested that hierarchy was embedded in the City Crown urban form (Colistra 2023), with the glass monument towering over the community, acting as yet another superstructure (Whyte 1982):

> The entire [city] decreases in importance from above to below, similar to the way humans are differentiated from one another in their tendencies and by their nature. The architecture crystallizes this image of human stratification. (Taut 2009[1919])

But later in the book, Taut stated that architecture must leverage and reflect the spiritual component of an entire community rather than just its creator's vision. In fact, he recommended that the City Crown be built gradually through the generations, after the rest of the city has gelled (Whyte 1982). Perhaps the problem is that, as an architect, Taut prioritised the architectural image of the city over its economic base or sociopolitical dynamics, which may have interested the working classes (Colistra 2023). Also, a text so rife with mystical overtones and esoteric and hermetic symbolism was unlikely to appeal, or even be comprehensible, to the average person (Whyte 1982).

Women were not mentioned in the City Crown. However, Taut's other work indicates that he was aware of the feminist movement and believed that women (i.e. housewives) should collaborate with architects in designing the New Dwelling, based on new, "scientific" methods of household management. He ventured into streamlining the conventional layout of German flats, challenging traditional, inefficient norms. Many of his ideas were borrowed from the work of a female writer, Christine Frederick. By advocating a reduction in space standards without compromising convenience, Taut sought to contribute innovative solutions to the housing crisis during times of national reconstruction. However, as commendable as his ideas were, criticism arose from the inherent middle-class assumptions embedded in Taut's approach. The allocation of specific activities to distinct rooms and the emphasis on 'privacy' were disconnected from the realities of what dwellings working-class households could afford. Furthermore, the cost implications of Taut's proposals raised concerns, not only among poorer communities but also within the middle class (Bullock 1988).

Le Corbusier's Cité Radieuse

Charles-Édouard Jeanneret, known as Le Corbusier (1887–1965), is probably the most famous among the authors discussed here. He is one of the few whose work has been formerly critiqued from a feminist perspective. Le Corbusier laid out his utopian vision for a 'Cité Radieuse' ('Radiant City') in a 1933 book, republished nearly verbatim in 1964. The Radiant City is a fascinating blend of contradictory ideas, reflecting the complexity of the architect himself. The book's tone is notably assertive, even bordering on arrogant. The author positions himself as the authoritative figure, dictating the correct way of living and unveiling what he perceives as the right path for urban development (Carranza 1994). He advocates for sweeping changes with a certain level of disdain for existing structures and societal norms. The language is exalted: passionate declarations are marked by exclamation points.

The Radiant City is expansive and metropolitan. The target density is quite high at 1,000 people per hectare, with everyone living in high-rises to leave ground space free for pedestrians to roam (Figure 7). While critical of Ebenezer Howard's Garden City concept, Le Corbusier's city echoes some aspects of a Garden City in the sense that it incorporates vast parks on the ground and green roofs with trees, sand, and water. Radiant City's transport system involves a radical restructuring of urban spaces. Le Corbusier proposes an elevated highway network, designed in a 400 × 400 metre grid, and elevated more than 20 metres off the ground. This airborne system, featuring wide roads, would separate pedestrians from most mechanical transportation.

Figure 7 Model of the Plan Voisin for Paris, based on the Cité Radieuse principles. Source: SiefkinDR. Licence CC BY-SA 4.0.

Tramways would run at street level beneath the elevated highway system. The plan also incorporates extensive parking lots suspended above ground at the fifth-floor level. The city would have no conventional streets in which different activities co-mingled. Pedestrians would have exclusive access to ground-level spaces (Le Corbusier 1964 [1933]).

Ideologically, Le Corbusier's vision combines seemingly incompatible elements of libertarianism and socialism. He advocates for individual freedom, and the Radiant City features a high-rise central business district not unlike those seen in the United States (but not in Europe) in the early twentieth century. At the same time, Le Corbusier proposes laws to regulate land values for public interest. At one point, he goes as far as claiming that all urban land should be held in public ownership. Moreover, Le Corbusier likes the idea of a patriarchal authority ("the plan") and a despot (presumably a male planner) to implement his vision. This reveals a fascination for the centralised authority he had seen while consulting in the Soviet Union but also his admiration for the Roman Empire. In his book, he emphasises the conquest of the world and the disciplined, hierarchical, geometric, and dignified nature of Roman cities. This admiration extends to the Roman military camp – the ultimate masculine space.

Le Corbusier's stance on egalitarianism is similarly complex. While relentlessly criticising the bourgeois consumerism of the so-called machine age, Le Corbusier's vision involves razing to the ground and rebuilding entire cities

– including Paris – casting doubt on his non-materialistic intentions. The apartments he designs are efficient and machine-like, minimising possessions and furniture and standardising all aspects of living. Certain elements of his apartment buildings, such as communal services, seem inclusive. However, these would wipe out myriad small businesses, such as eateries, which may have provided women with an income. Also, his proposal to separate functions within the city, assigning specific zones to different groups (e.g. workers and administrators), suggests a hierarchical approach that contradicts the idea of true egalitarianism (Hooper 2002). At times he cannot conceal his condescension towards the poorer and less educated segments of the population. He even claims that only a select group would be capable of "entering the spirit of his buildings," understanding and embracing his architectural intentions.

With regard to gender, Le Corbusier's Radiant City, as well as his vision and oeuvre more broadly, reflect a deeply ingrained sexism within his architectural philosophy. In essence, his understanding of masculinity and femininity is binary and oppositional: men are the "sun" (active, powerful, and dominant), whereas women are "water" (passive, fluid, nurturing). His portrayal of women is objectifying. Le Corbusier's drawings subject women to voyeuristic gazes, reinforcing traditional gender stereotypes (Carranza 1994). Also, women are often positioned in socially prescribed roles, such as in the kitchen. The architect's obsession with efficiency and minimalistic living translates into a disregard for the practical needs and privacy concerns of women. For example, for no convincing reason, he proposes that apartment buildings be enclosed in transparent and airtight glass walls rather than having traditional windows and curtains. Despite expressing some concern for women's well-being by eliminating the need for heavy shopping and daily cooking through deliveries and laundries (Samuel 2004), Le Corbusier's vision ultimately limits women to traditional domestic roles. Another interesting theme in the Radiant City is Le Corbusier's obsession with sports and physical prowess. This is tied to his vision of revitalising the male body, making it a thing of magnificence (Hooper 2002).

Le Corbusier's views on the relationships between men and women reflect both progressive and traditional elements. On the one hand, he acknowledges the strains in relationships caused by the contemporary lifestyle, where men and women are separated for extended periods due to work, leading to alienation. He identifies the crushing domestic duties on women as a factor contributing to this alienation and hindering genuine connection. In an attempt to address these issues, Le Corbusier proposes reductions in work time for both men and women. He advocates for limiting men's job schedules and women's domestic work to five hours per day. This reduction aims to provide more leisure time and opportunities for men and women to be together, fostering improved relationships. However, women remain the centre of home and family life (Samuel 2004).

In the 'Radiant City', Le Corbusier talks about the wife of the cook of his Brazilian friend ("the king of Brazilian coffee"), a short, overweight woman fascinated by cinema. This woman was so captivated by the city lights portrayed in the films that she left her husband for Los Angeles in pursuit of her Hollywood dream. Le Corbusier uses this anecdote to illustrate how even this "simpleton" found the allure of city life irresistible. This anecdote is supposed to strengthen Le Corbusier's argument that the future will be cosmopolitan. Yet, it reveals the architect's disdain for women (as well as the poor).

Le Corbusier's work is sexist from a stylistic, as well as a functional, perspective. His emphasis on the masculine is starkly evident in his fixation on pure geometric forms, the glorification of the Modular Man, and a mechanistic view of architecture (Bersky 2013). His preference for clean lines, straight angles, and rigid geometric shapes reflects a desire for order and rationality – characteristics often associated with the male gender. The Radiant City plan itself is positioned as mastery over nature, whereas ornamentation and curves are associated with the feminine. So is chaos and decay: old Paris is referred to as "she." Le Corbusier's famous statement, "The naked man for me is architecture; when I no longer make architecture, I see everything as women," further underscores his reduction of architectural prowess to a masculine identity (Hooper 2002).

In the real world, Le Corbusier's ideas were applied through master plans and site designs. In Algiers, his massive ribbons contrasted with the intricate fabric of the Arabic city. In Stockholm, he was more restrained, using the historic city as a departure point for his plan. Perhaps the most advanced application of his vision was in Chandigarh – the new, post-colonial capital of the Punjab region in northern India (Pojani 2021). Overall, Le Corbusier's work illustrates his commitment to what he terms the "surgical principle" of urban planning. As a major architectural personality, he was often given free rein. Fortunately, the practical realities of the cities and sites in which he worked prevented him from implementing his macho utopias in full.

Antonio Sant'Elia's Città Nuova

An Italian architect, Antonio Sant'Elia (1888–1916) was a key figure in the Futurist movement, which celebrated speed, technology, and the modern age. His major contribution is an urban concept known as 'Città Nuova' or 'New City', which was first presented at an exhibition by the group 'Tendenze Nuove' in 1914. Sant'Elia's ideas were documented in six drawings as well as a four-page 'Manifesto of Futurist Architecture', which he co-signed. His 1911 self-portrait, in which he presents himself as a modern man prototype, is composed in the angular and dynamic style of Futurism.

In line with modernism, Sant'Elia's work had an ideological function: it aimed to challenge existing architectural norms and inspire innovative thinking. Futurists like Sant'Elia regarded much of Italy as a backward country in dire need of reform. They were enthralled by the myth of American architecture – specifically New York's (Birolli 2016). Sant'Elia worked in Milan, which was at the forefront of Italian industrialisation efforts. This had a profound impact on his thinking about urban spaces and architecture (Budzynski 2016).

Sant'Elia's career was rather short. Out of his projects, a single villa was ever built. A lifelong socialist, he enlisted in the army during World War I. At that moment, youth shared a belief that the war would bring about a new era of modernity and societal transformation; the artistic avant-garde was aligned with the military vanguard (Budzynski 2016). While Sant'Elia lost his life in combat in 1916, he has been highly influential in twentieth-century urban design theory and discourse.

Sant'Elia's Città Nuova was a series of urban fragments rather than a fully formed city. It featured towering skyscrapers made of modern materials like concrete, glass, and steel (Figure 8). Like Haussmann in the previous century (see page 36), Sant'Elia advocated a clean slate approach, an elimination of existing elements, including major historic monuments, that no longer fit the requirements of modern society. Sant'Elia also shared Tony Garnier's fascination with electricity and electric power plants (see page 18), and emphasised the rational and scientific use of materials in urban development. However, the Città Nuova, a densely populated metropolis, is the conceptual opposite of Garnier's self-sufficient and verdant town concept. Sant'Elia's 12- to 20-storey-high terraced houses are served by external elevators that climb up the facades like mechanical serpents. He saw height as a precondition to overcoming the limitations of urban space and sought to combine large-scale housing standards with individual needs for space and comfort. However, an emphasis on grandiosity, heroism, and power can also be associated with masculine ideals of dominance and control.

Sant'Elia's designs also highlighted the importance of transport and movement within the city, which he saw as necessary to accommodate the rapid pace of modern life. He conceptualised future urban environments as constantly changing and dynamic. Like Le Corbusier, Sant'Elia talked about the city as a well-oiled machine, functional and efficient (Birolli 2016). This focus on mechanisation echoes traditional masculine associations with machinery and technology. Sant'Elia also disdained historical continuity and

Figure 8 Multi-family building. Source: Wikimedia Commons. Image in the public domain.

unnecessary ornamentation, typically associated with feminine sentimentality. Instead, he advocated for a complete break with traditional styles. This minimalist approach supports masculine ideals of simplicity and efficiency but can also be seen as a refusal of bourgeois values and stylistic preferences in nineteenth-century Milan (Caramel and Longatti 1988).

Sant'Elia's Città Nuova, like Le Corbusier's Radiant City, appears to be born out of nothing (Budzynski 2016). Some of the buildings in his architectural drawings take on a spiritual quality, owing to the use of deep shadows, violent colours, dark contours, and bottom-up perspectives (Caramel and Longatti 1988). However, this is a more abstract or contemporary spirituality, distinct from traditional Italian Catholicism.

While formally innovative, Sant'Elia's New City is not envisioned as a women- and family-friendly place. Humans are nearly absent from his drawings. Indeed, humans are apparently unwelcome in Sant'Elia's technological cityscapes. Where any inhabitants are shown, they appear as tiny black dots squeezed between titanic buildings. The city has no gardens, piazzas, theatres, or schools (Budzynski 2016). This reflects a focus on architectural form at the expense of people. Images of women's bodies are sometimes used in façade decorations, but there is a grotesque effect in the distortion of their shapes, their swollen bellies, and graceless limbs (Caramel and Longatti 1988). This raises questions about the representation of gender in his vision of the future city. Seen through a feminist lens, Sant'Elia's New City appears as an unhinged fantasy seeking to glorify the machine age. His work was adept at creating discursive schemata for the modern city but not a liveable city blueprint (Birolli 2016).

Nikolay Milyutin's Sotsgorod

Nikolay Milyutin (1889–1942) was a Soviet functionary, later turned architectural critic and planning theorist. He was one of a series of "administrator-visionaries, bureaucrat-enthusiasts, who performed government work with great dedication and an apparent dose of lunacy" (Vujosevic 2017: 68). His book, Sotsgorod (a portmanteau meaning 'socialist city'), was written in the late 1920s, while debates were raging in the USSR about socialist urban form and content. The Sotsgorod model was selected for inclusion here because it embodies the radical sociopolitical creed of that time and place.[3] It is a city engendered by production rather than consumption (i.e. trade and mercantilism). Milyutin is one of the few authors considered here who mention women specifically.

While his book postdated the Bolshevik Party's land socialisation decree by more than two decades (Collins 1974), Sotsgorod shows clear links with models such as 'the linear city' and 'the industrial city' which were emerging in the West at the time under conditions of private land ownership. This is not surprising. Trotskyist authors – see Cliff and Harman (1974) – have argued that the Soviet Union was not a "workers' state" but rather a version of bureaucratic state capitalism. It resembled industrial capitalism in that both systems involved large-scale industrial production, centralised control of economic activity, pricing as a means to allocate resources, and appalling work conditions for men and women alike.

Milyutin proposed a linear plan for an industrial settlement extending along transport infrastructures (road and rail). All functions were separated into six parallel bands, which were to be laid out in a fixed sequence and could extend, potentially endlessly, on either side as the city grew (Figure 9). The industrial plant itself was also strip-like, drawing inspiration from the

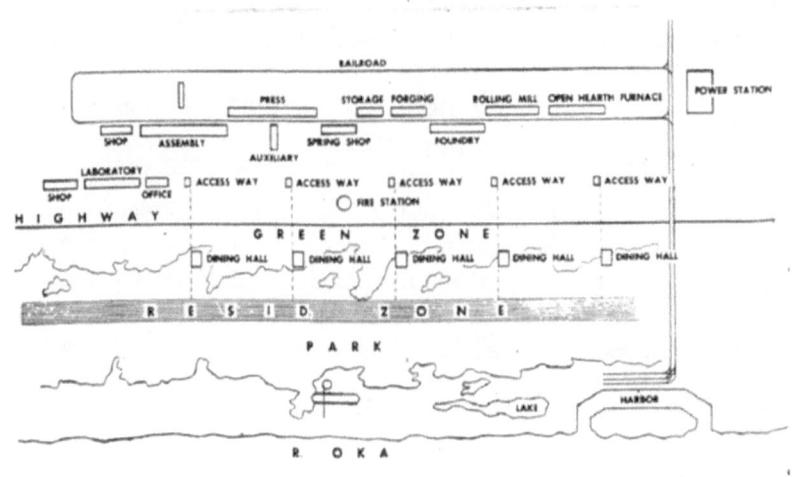

Figure 9 Linear city plan for an auto plant. Source: Image by Azmah Arzmi. Licence: CC BY-ND 4.0.

Fordist assembly line system. This concept differed from Garnier's and Le Corbusier's arrangement of functions into clusters (see pages 18 and 23). It had the advantage of insulating residences from noise and smoke by a green ribbon while minimising the commuting distances for workers. The assumption was that one could find housing in the portion of the residential band that was nearest the portion of the industrial band where one was employed (and would be prepared to move in the case of a change in employment). This setup was likely to create transient residential spaces, which lacked the sense of belonging experienced in the countryside. However, it provided the government with an effective way to control and discipline the population (Vujosevic 2017).

Overall, Milyutin's plan showcased a vision for a socialist industrialised landscape, which would presumably eliminate traditional distinctions between urban and rural life and liberate peasant women from the patriarchal yoke. His designs marked a departure from the monumentality and grandeur of imperial Russia in favour of industrial efficiency and modularity (Collins 1974). He highlighted the savings inherent in simple, low-rise buildings (factories or residences) and openly decried skyscrapers as "the last cry of capitalism." (Miliutin 2021[1930]: 149) Topography was largely irrelevant in Sotsgorod. With regard to architecture, Milyutin advocated for modernisation, streamlining, and lightweight materials, based strictly on the Bauhaus style. To support his approach, Milyutin interspersed his writings with quotes from Marx, Engels, Lenin, and Stalin.

Central to Milyutin's vision was the concept of the "living cell," a basic residential unit of 8.4 square metres designed as an ascetic hotel room with a single bed, a table, and a shelf. Practically, this domestic environment resembled a mechanism, with the foldable furniture requiring some effort to operate. Workers were expected to use this cell for lonesome activities such as sleep, rest, or reading, whereas eating and socialising would take place in collective buildings such as canteens, clubs, cinemas, and libraries. Individual cooking, washing, mending, and caretaking would be replaced by communal kitchens, laundries, repair shops, and clinics for which detailed statistics were provided.

These facilities and services – located separately from residences for hygiene reasons – were intended to (a) phase out the family as a bourgeois economic unit meant for the accumulation of property and possessions, and (b) release women from "barbaric" housework in the service of husbands and children. Marriage itself was challenged as a form of socially accepted prostitution, whereas promiscuity was tolerated, if not always appreciated by women (Vujosevic 2017). Milyutin said about the marital bed: "One cannot but regret that in certain circles of our party, the bourgeois ideology is so strong, that, with a diligence worthy of a less petty purpose, they think up ever new arguments for retaining the double bed as a permanent and compulsory item in the worker's home!" (Miliutin 2021[1930]: 47). Instead of having spouses share a bed, he envisioned two unrelated individuals in adjacent living cells sharing a bathroom (Vujosevic 2017).

Sotsgorod's pre-school children were assigned not only to daytime nurseries but also to nighttime dormitories. Milyutin fretted that "placing nurseries and kindergartens in dwellings breeds epidemics among children" (Miliutin 2021[1930]: 52). At the same time, experiments with motherhood in that era went as far as entailing collective breastfeeding, so that Soviet children would become "brothers in milk" (Vujosevic 2017). However, Milyutin acknowledged the importance of parent-child relationships and conceded that young children should not be altogether barred from seeing their parents. Older children were expected to participate in productive labour activities in addition to receiving instruction and partaking in gymnastics, in order to strengthen their bodies and their minds to better serve the party but also to free up mothers' time to work outside the home. An underlying message was that socialist women did not need husbands for childrearing; children would be taken care of by their "collective father, Stalin" (Vujosevic 2017: 133).

In the book, Milyutin appeared to be genuinely concerned about women's emancipation, welfare, and their equal participation in Soviet society. However, as a former government administrator, he was also motivated by a need to (1) boost workforce numbers and overall productivity in impoverished Soviet cities and (2) contain rural-urban migration by male workers which was intensifying major housing shortages in cities. It is important not to forget that in the Soviet era, the design of the built environment remained the purview of male architects and planners (Vujosevic 2017).

While Milyutin's plan was utopian and later faced resistance from other party ideologues, it did have an influence on planning practice in the Soviet Union. For example, Molotov, a new revolutionary town, started as a workers' community built in accordance with Sotsgorod principles. In the 1930s, as Soviet society turned more conservative and family-oriented, some of the extreme ideas of the post-Revolution period were abandoned. Architecture returned to classicism and eclecticism. The state continued to protect mothers and children by providing (tiny) housing and childcare facilities but also introduced new legislation which banned abortion and made divorce very difficult. Milyutin's Modernist designs were not rediscovered until the Khrushchev era in the 1960s (Collins 1974).

The Rational Functionalists

The rational functionalists embraced the logic of progress, technology, and efficiency. They aimed to reshape the urban landscape based on functional needs, prioritising utility and the demands of industrial society. For this group, modernity represented a necessary and welcome break from a stifling past.

Titus Salt's and George Pullman's model mill towns

Titus Salt (1803–1876) was an English industrialist who designed and built a model factory employing over 3,500 men, women, and children in northern England, and a nearby town called Saltaire (after him) to house his workforce. Having operated textile manufacturing plants since the 1830s, Salt was concerned about the levels of penury, alcoholism, lawlessness, and unsanitary living among the working classes. He believed that one solution was to move away from densely populated cities and start new, industrial communities on greenfield sites connected to other places via train. Developed in the mid- to late 1800s, Saltaire was one of the earliest large-scale mill towns in Britain initiated by a private individual. It has long been considered a landmark example of enlightened nineteenth-century urban planning (Cherry 1979), and it is inscribed on the UNESCO World Heritage list. At completion, it covered an area of twenty-five acres (Balgarnie 1878) and included over 850 houses (Dewhirst 1960).

Saltaire had a simple grid plan with two major axes, which were lined with the institutions of everyday life, including a workers' canteen/shop, infirmary, mausoleum, almshouses, baths, churches, schools, clubs, parks, and allotment gardens (Markus 2003). The town was designed in Neo-Renaissance style. The mill itself was set within walking distance of most homes (Figure 10). Well-ventilated and well-lit education facilities were provided for boys and girls, segregated by gender and age. Boys' playgrounds were equipped with gym appliances (Holroyd 1871). By the late 1870s, a nursery (infant school) was set up to free female workers from childcare, as well as to allow them to work. Notably, the city contained no public drinking houses (Ashworth 1954). Housing was certainly of high quality relative to the typical worker's cottage in England. And sanitary conditions were far superior to what was available elsewhere at the time. One contemporaneous commentator hailed the communal bathing and washing facilities:

> The baths and washhouses contain two plunge baths, twenty-four warm baths, and Turkish and douche baths; forty-eight washing, rinsing, and steam tubs; forty-eight drying closets, hydro extractors, mangles and all other requisites: the charges made are little more than nominal. (Holroyd 1871: 12,18–19)

Figure 10 Aerial view of Saltaire. Source: Wellcome Trust. Licence: CC BY 4.0.

However, these facilities were to be used individually. Feminist notions of cooperative housekeeping did not apply in Saltaire – although cooking facilities and space were made available in the workers' canteen for individuals who wished to prepare their food in those spaces (Balgarnie 1878). While Salt was a great philanthropist who donated to many good causes, by some accounts, he also had a controlling personality in regard to the personal uses of space by his workers. Householders were prevented from hanging their laundry in their backyards, and Salt used to personally inspect people's yards and cut any laundry lines with his sabre (Greed 1994). Washing, presumably done by the female residents not working in the mills, needed to be carried to the centralised wash and dry facilities (Balgarnie 1878).

It has been argued that the motivation to establish Saltaire was a mix of Christian duty, economic efficiency, and a mechanism to control the proletariat (Ashworth 1954). A religious man, Salt sought to bring about social and moral reform by addressing not only the housing needs of his "most deserving" workers but also controlling their educational, moral, and personal conduct (British Heritage 2016). Only disciplined workers of good moral standing were provided with an old-age pension. (State pensions were introduced decades later in Britain.) Salt's economic reforms supported male dominance: only male workers were assisted in obtaining mortgages to buy their dwellings (Ashworth 1954). Employees included young children selected from students attending his factory schools (Dishman 2020). If any workers left the mill, they would lose their home too and face an uncertain future. Seen in this light, Saltaire and other mill towns are revealed as a top-down attempt to mould the lives of the working class. Salt Mills remained in operation until the 1980s.

Across the Atlantic, a similar development was Pullman, a mill town on the outskirts of Chicago, created in the early 1880s (Figure 11) by a wealthy industrialist, George Pullman (1831–1897), who made his money building luxury railway cars.[4] This town was promoted as a model in urban planning and industrial organisation until 1894 when its residents initiated one of America's most significant labour strikes. From social rules of behaviour to urban planning and architecture, every aspect of the settlement was carefully designed. Pullman shared Salt's belief that planned changes in physical environments could bring about positive social change (Baxter 2012). However, he was less motivated by philanthropic ideals than by the prospect of increasing worker productivity and receiving a favourable rate of return from his investments in housing and public facilities (Buder 1966).

By building a model mill town, Pullman wanted to physically demonstrate the interdependence of capitalism and labour (Baxter 2012). In his view, industrialisation need not lead to overcrowding and social disintegration (Buder

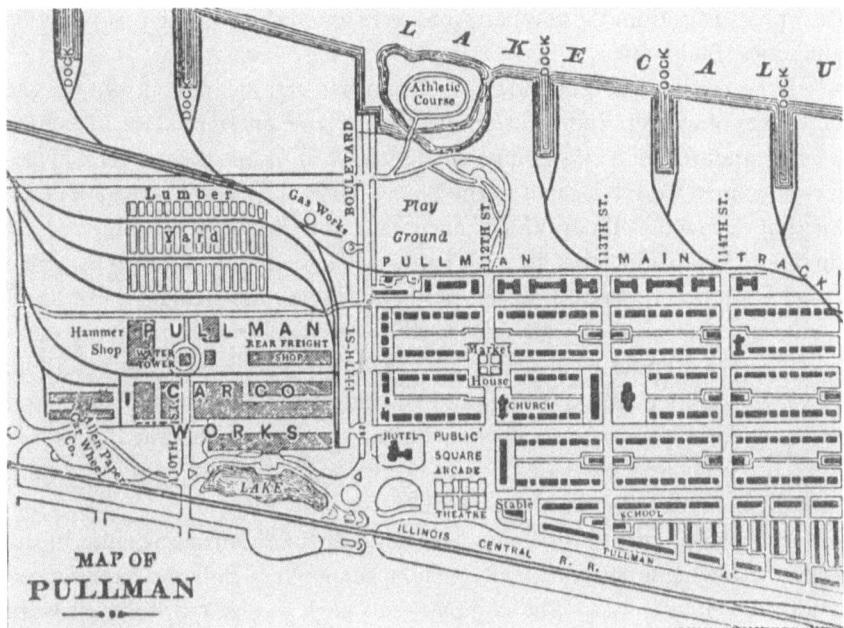

Figure 11 Map of Pullman. Source: *Harper's Magazine*. Image in the public domain.

1966). By offering steady work, ordered public spaces, adequate houses, and schools for children, the company sought to attract a "conscientious, contented, and skilled" male workforce (Reiff and Hirsch 1989). In contrast to Salt's Christian calling, Pullman openly admitted that "there was nothing benevolent in his motivations" (Hoover 1988: 18).

Pullman was built on a sparsely populated site of about three-hundred acres facing a lake. A broad belt of company land encircling the factory and settlement was left undeveloped, in order to spatially separate the new town from the city of Chicago. (Buder 1966). The plan was simple and linear, stretching between the lake shore and the railroad line. As the town grew, residential areas were extended. A park, hotel, church, and the 'Arcade' (a shopping and community centre) greeted people arriving at the train station in the town. The residential streets were tree-lined with small front yards (Buder 1966). The housing was designed to accommodate different levels of employees, with distinct neighbourhoods, designs, and fittings for various social strata. Executives lived closest to the main public buildings and parks, whereas unskilled workers' homes were located on the fringes, farther from Pullman Works and public spaces (Baxter 2012). Workers rented their properties from the company and were asked to cover the cost of public amenities (Buder 1966).

As the landlord and employer, Pullman had significant control over the daily lives of workers and their families. All were required to abide by behavioural standards set by the company (Buder 1966). While men worked in factories, women were relegated to the home. Their duty was to create a home life that reflected Pullman Works' corporate values and provided rest, moral direction, and pacification for male workers. Men were encouraged to return home for lunch cooked by wives, mothers, sisters, and daughters. In addition to cooking, women were expected to "bear children and nurture them in the habits of industry, frugality and above all cleanliness" (Hoover 1998: 319,321). The population of Pullman was predominately young, white, and male (Buder 1966). In accordance with the customs of the era, Blacks had limited job choices, were paid lower wages, were spatially segregated, and verbally abused (Pullman Museum 2020).

General discontent over living and working conditions grew, and, in the 1890s, following a nationwide depression, the town of Pullman experienced a socio-economic crisis. The company cut back wages and hours of work and laid off workers – which led to unemployment, hunger, and eventually a large-scale workers' strike in May 1894 (Reiff 1997). The strike brought the mill and town to an end. Practically, it "served to emphasize the commercial basis of the town, to expose Pullman's lack of genuine interest in the welfare of labour, and to magnify the inherent weakness of the Pullman experiment" (Lindsey 1939, cited in Hoover 1988: 101). In 1907, the City of Chicago annexed Pullman.

Georges-Eugène Haussmann and the transformation of Paris

A powerful public administrator, Baron Georges-Eugène Haussmann (1809–1891), is renowned for transforming Paris into a grand city of wide boulevards, star-shaped plazas, and imposing buildings. His ambitious project was initiated in response to Emperor Napoléon III's desire to modernise the overcrowded and unsanitary capital and bring it in line with its competitor, London. Napoléon III appointed Haussmann as Prefect of the Seine in 1853, a post he retained until 1870 (Freemark et al. 2022). Haussmann's trusted director of public works was an engineer, Adolphe Alphand, who later published all the technical drawings produced during his tenure in an epic catalogue containing more than 550 illustrations – of street sections, plans, perspectives, urban furniture detailing, and so on (Alphand 1867). (See Figure 12 for an example.)

Figure 12 Plan, profile, and urban furniture of Avenue de l'Impératrice (now Avenue Foch). Source: Musée Carnavalet. Licence: CC0 1.0.

More than a century after his death, Baron Haussmann remains a highly controversial figure in planning history. Opinions in France and abroad remain sharply divided as to whether Haussmann was a visionary planner or a ruthless autocrat (Willsher 2016). On the one hand, he is credited as the driving force behind a swift public works programme – unprecedented in scale – which came to define the City of Light. According to supporters, under Haussmann's helm, Paris became a healthier, more organised, and aesthetically appealing capital city (Figure 13). They argue that the expropriation, clearance, and construction of housing under the Second Empire were motivated by a genuine interest in providing a greater quantity and quality of shelter at reduced costs; in fact, the new construction exceeded what was destroyed (see Freemark et al. 2022). In addition to improvements above ground, Haussmann's project also encompassed the installation of an extensive underground network of water and sewer lines, which the city desperately needed (Willsher 2016).

On the flip side, Haussmann and his patron, Napoléon III, have been accused of obliterating the historic charm of medieval Paris, using eminent domain powers to clear slums for the purpose of separating the rich from the poor and making space for upscale housing. To detractors, the broad public spaces served not to embellish Paris but to quell social dissent and aid the military in suppressing popular uprisings (Willsher 2016). It has also been contended that, historically, an inclination towards symmetry and order has

Figure 13 Aerial view of Avenue des Champs-Élysées and other newly created avenues and boulevards. Source: Musée Carnavalet. Licence: CC0 1.0.

corresponded to despotic governments because a symmetrical arrangement facilitates surveillance and domination from a single point (Frisby 2003).

Furthermore, critics contend that the interventions carried out during the Second Empire led to social stratifications in Paris. The displacement of poor residents from the city centre resulted in profound and, some argue, intentional consequences. Major interventions were said to stimulate and rely upon a wealthier consumer class, consolidating property ownership among large-scale landlords and transforming once-packed low-income neighbourhoods into attractive bourgeois communities. This socio-economic shift had a lasting impact on spatialised economic inequalities that persist today (Freemark et al. 2022).

Feminist commentators have argued that Haussmannisation was, at its essence, a disciplinary planning strategy that sought to separate not only "incompatible" urban functions (such as work and living, public and private space) but also "incompatible" humans, such as rich and poor and men and women (Hooper 1998). The public sphere gradually came to symbolise the realms of labour, politics, and education, predominantly associated with men. While Haussmannisation spurred the boulevardier/flâneur phenomenon

(Jordan 1992), this activity was also reserved for men. Meanwhile, activities performed by working-class women, such as laundry and street vending, that once took place in the open along the river and streets, were relocated to enclosed, specialised locations (markets and laundries). Haussmann's apartment buildings no longer reserved ground floors for shops, and zoning practices further isolated residential neighbourhoods from businesses, reinforcing the separation of domestic (feminine) space from commercial (masculine) exchange (Marcus 2001). Possibly, a need to control women via planning and architectural devices was a reaction to a perceived loss of masculinity associated with apartment living, which contrasted with the patriarchal lifestyles that had prevailed in the family houses of rural areas (Marcus 2001).

A lesser-known but revealing aspect of the story is that the dust generated by Haussmann's works for decades imposed a societal need for women to wear veils covering their faces outdoors (Figure 14). Although working-class women were more affected by pollution and disease, the medical community's directives focused on bourgeois women. The veil literally restricted those women's fields of vision and symbolically reinforced the idea that a clean and healthy woman (and her home) was a mirror of respectability and moral goodness. Ironically, the veiling fashion came at a time when sidewalk improvements

Figure 14 Photograph of public works around the Trocadéro. Source: Musée Carnavalet. Licence: CC0 1.0.

had reduced the earlier messiness of strolling. Possibly, fears of physical and social contagion were intensified because the destruction of former locales for brothels and the prohibitive rents in redeveloped districts contributed to the visibility of sex workers on the streets. The bourgeois apartments in Haussmann's new buildings were equipped with balconies so that occupants could observe life below without fear of contamination (Kessler 2005).

Opposition to Haussmann's plans was vehement, with major discontent fuelled by displacement but also by the massive expenditure for the reconstruction (Willsher 2016). Mounting criticism tarnished Haussmann's reputation, as well as undermined Emperor Napoléon III's popularity, eventually forcing him to dismiss the Prefect. The Second Empire collapsed soon after (Willsher 2016). Following his fall from grace, Haussmann spent his retirement writing a voluminous memoir. First published in 1890, this memoir is only available in French, but several biographies, which rely heavily on his memoir, have been written in or translated into English (see Jordan 1995; Weeks 1999; Carmona 2002).

The memoir provides a window into Haussmann's personality and inner thoughts. His prose has been characterised as lacking elegance and artfulness. Embittered, he portrays his career as filled with adversity and blames his misfortunes on others, presenting himself as capable, innovative, forthright, and principled, showing little interest in self-examination or self-criticism (Jordan 1992; Freemark et al. 2022). He proudly declared that in less than five years he had "disembowelled" an entire area known for uprisings and barricades. Haussmann's mindset was focused on function and utility, with an obsessive need for order and detail, cataloguing details extensively in his writings. Apparently, even the emperor had expressed concerns about Haussmann's obsession with straight lines for the newly created streets. Overall, Haussmann appears as an old-fashioned figure, seeking to justify and glorify himself and his master – and thus, indirectly, the state (Jordan 1992).

Ildefons Cerdà and Barcelona's Eixample plan

Ildefons Cerdà (1815–1876) is considered the pioneer of rational-comprehensive planning, even deemed a 'planning genius' in his native Spain and further afield. One Spanish commentator describes him thus:

> Cerdà helped bring about momentous change, turning 19th-century Spain from a country of cramped cities burdened by the weight of history into one of new, spacious cities, intent on recognizing and celebrating the complexity of urbanization processes, which this unique

engineer introduced into the habits of the time, as though they were quite natural. (Martín-Ramos 2012: 695)

Cerdà's crowning achievements include (a) his 1855 survey of Barcelona; (b) his 1859 project for the expansion of Barcelona beyond the Old City walls into an area called the Eixample; and (c) his magnum opus, 'General Theory of Urbanization', published in 1867. Cerdà is, in fact, credited with having coined the term 'urbanización', which he defined as "a set of tenets, principles, doctrines, and rules intended to demonstrate how groups of buildings should be ordered so that they fulfil their purpose, which can be summarised as ensuring the inhabitants can live comfortably with the ability to provide services to one another, thus contributing to the general welfare" (Cerdà 2017[1867]: 69).

Born into a minor aristocratic family, Cerdà's upbringing was marked by a blend of progressive influences. His engineering education at the Escuela de Ingenieros de Caminos in Madrid instilled in him the virtues of rationalism and liberalism.[5] His involvement in the Milicia Nacional voluntary troops also exposed him to progressive and humanistic ideologies, as well as working-class concerns. However, Cerdà was no communist. He saw poorly constructed, crowded worker housing in Barcelona's Old City as a "training school for communism" (Soria y Puig 1995). In his writings, he expressed a strong commitment to individual liberty, which he linked to the physical independence and privacy of (male) individuals and families. To him, the ideal living situation involved dwellings on separate lots, with setbacks on all sides, but he acknowledged such housing was largely unfeasible in Barcelona's reality (Hermansen-Cordua 2010).

Above all, Cerdà conceived of himself as a Renaissance man. He dabbled in moral philosophy, architecture, social studies, statistics, hygiene, law, property, politics, economics, finance, geography, and public administration in addition to urban planning, civil engineering, and transportation (Aibar and Bijker 1997). He embarked on the planning of a new Barcelona to accommodate the city's industrial growth in the mid-nineteenth century. He saw the existing city structure as inadequate for an expanding population and the changing needs of an industrial society. Despite the dire living conditions of male and female workers, he perceived the nineteenth century as a transformative era, characterised by movement, communication, and technological progress, and was essentially optimistic about the future of humanity.

Prior to drafting the extension plan for Barcelona, Cerdà conducted meticulous surveys and statistical analyses of Barcelona. These were pivotal in introducing a scientific and techno-rational approach to urban planning, somewhat similar to the approach of Otto Wagner in Vienna (see page 44).

Cerdà sought to understand the fundamental aspects of the city – its physical elements, population, housing conditions, and economic dynamics. In particular, he aimed to quantify and understand the living conditions of working-class families. However, his calculations emphasised male wage earners. Cerdà operated under the assumption, which would later become common, that the male head of the household was the main contributor to the family's income, with women's wages considered supplementary. This approach reinforced the societal norms and gender divisions of the time (Borderías and López-Guallar 2001).

The Barcelona *Eixample* (extension) plan was initially unsolicited. Cerdà voluntarily presented a draft to a magazine. The plan featured a grid-based layout covering 22 blocks, intersected by two diagonal avenues (Figure 15). The Old Town was marginalised at the periphery of the plan. The streets were extra wide: 35 metres, later reduced to 20 metres, out of financial necessity. But even in the final plan, roads covered over 30 per cent of the total area, which was very high for the time. The 45-degree chamfered street corners were designed to facilitate better traffic flow (by allowing for smoother turns and intersections). The spaces isolated by the street network were referred to as 'intrevías' (inter-ways) rather than blocks. Cerdà also proposed an extensive network of underground infrastructure, including provisions

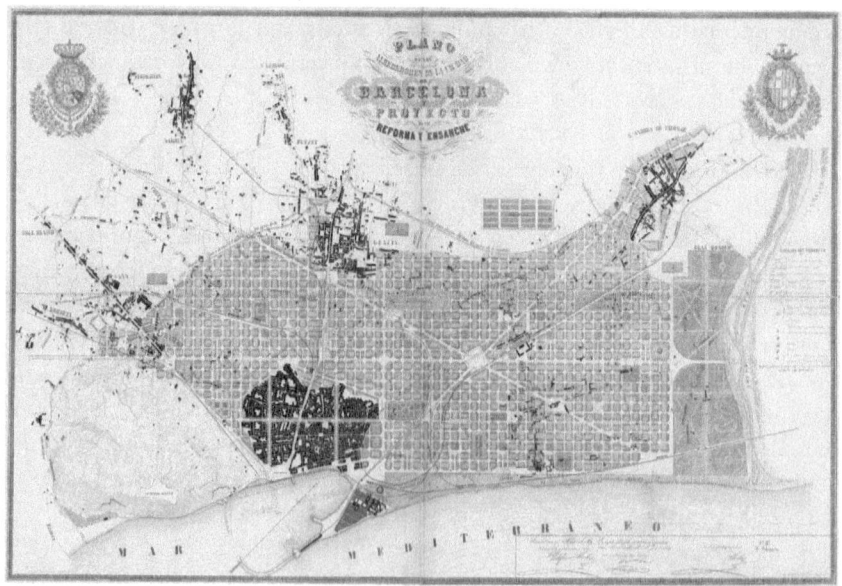

Figure 15 Enlargement map of Barcelona. Source: Museu d'Historia de la Ciutat. Image in the public domain.

for sewerage and storm drainage. In combination, these features highlighted Cerdà's engineering predisposition and his focus on transport, speed, and mechanised movement. Later, Cerdà was praised for anticipating a world where movement was essential, where cities would expand and transform due to the increasing demand for space, comfort, and rapid circulation (Neuman 2011; Hermansen-Cordua 2010). However, rather than foresight, in the twenty-first century this could be seen as a self-fulfilling prophecy.

On the positive side, Cerdà's plan also exhibited concern for the humans that would populate the Eixample. The plan incorporated public amenities, such as hospitals, markets, and social centres. The housing Cerdà designed was never taller than four storeys. Houses lined the block perimeters, forming street walls (which Le Corbusier came to despise decades later). To prevent homes from facing north and minimise shadow casting between blocks, the plan followed the northwest-southeast and northeast-southwest directions. Architectural elements like porticos and galleries were envisioned to protect pedestrians from extreme weather conditions. A significant portion of street width, around 10 metres, was allocated for sidewalks and street furniture. All blocks incorporated open green spaces on one or more sides so that residents could access light and air. To achieve fairness and equality in street prestige, the blocks were square rather than rectangular. The block size (113.3 square metres) was, however, derived from a mysterious formula. So was the standard of six cubic metres of air per person in each home. While obscure, these precise technical details served to appeal to other (male) engineers who liked the scientific and objective character associated with mathematics (Aibar and Bijker 1997).

Cerdà's plan faced significant opposition and challenges from various quarters. The Barcelona council, as well as local architects, expressed concerns over the plan's limitless scope, its financial implications from expropriations, and its scientific as opposed to artistic underpinnings. The council even proposed a competing radial extension plan, which stemmed from the Old City nucleus. Cerdà's forceful personality and influential connections, notably his ties to the central government in Madrid, played a pivotal role in overcoming this resistance and obtaining approval for his plan. He devoted much of his career to the implementation of the plan – either as an elected politician or as a technical adviser.

As the Eixample was being built, Cerdà devoted himself to writing his book *General Theory of Urbanization*.[6] In the book, Cerdà applies a medical and scientific language to urban settings, writing about "dissecting" cities and societies and pointing to poor planning as the fundamental cause of societal "ills". These linguistic choices were deliberate as he sought to earn a place for urban planning in the field of science, which was completely masculine at the time.

Construction work progressed with considerable controversy. A pragmatist, Cerdà made major concessions along the way. The practical implementation of the plan significantly favoured the bourgeoisie, despite the plan's stated egalitarian objectives. Ultimately, the working classes were relegated to dilapidated peripheries or remained in the crumbling Old City (Wynn 1979). This could have been predicted because, after all, Cerdà's approach to urbanisation, mirroring American city structures, reflected the rationalisation of space under capitalism, which is conducive to unfettered capital accumulation. His focus on technical interventions over broader social transformations and equity issues showcased a reductionist approach, considering urban and social issues primarily as public health problems to be solved through technical means (Aibar and Bijker 1997). While contemporary Barcelona still retains its block-based framework and chamfered street corners, the general impression is of a grand imperial city, jammed with car traffic.[7]

Otto Wagner's Die Grossstadt and Vienna's masterplan

Otto Wagner (1841–1918) was one of the leading architects and theorists of the Austro-Hungarian Empire. He lived and worked in Vienna during a period of significant urban development and change, known as the city's 'second renaissance' (Frisby 1997). A professor at the Imperial Academy of Fine Arts in Vienna, he authored the first treatise on modern architecture. This was later followed by a book called 'Die Grossstadt' (The Great City), of which only a short English-language summary is available (Wagner 1912). In the book, he reviewed urban planning issues first in general terms, then in reference to Vienna. A prolific architect, Wagner was part of the Secession movement, which represented a break from academic traditions and embraced modernism, including elements of Art Nouveau and Jugendstil. However, Wagner's style was much more rational, sober, and "masculine" than the ornate and extravagant designs of some other Secessionists (Geretsegger and Peintner 1970).

In 1893, Wagner won the competition for the general regulatory plan of Vienna. This achievement allowed him to implement his ideas and theories in practice. A central concept of the Secession movement was the idea of the 'Gesamtkunstwerk' (total work of art). In line with this concept, Wagner sought to integrate and homogenise the city of Vienna into a unitary whole. Before taking on the entire urban plan, he had worked on the Stadtbahn, the elevated ring-rail around Vienna, designing the lines, stations, and bridges (Figure 16). Hence his interest in transport and traffic, which became the generating element of the Vienna plan (Geretsegger and Peintner 1970).

Figure 16 Study for a subway stop entrance. Source: Anno. Image in the public domain.

Wagner's urban planning vision was metropolitan and expansive. Clear parallels can be drawn with the ideas of Georges-Eugène Haussmann for Paris, Ildefons Cerdà for Barcelona, and Daniel Burnham for Chicago, which were radically different from the self-contained visions of contemporaries like Ebenezer Howard and Tony Garnier. Wagner seemed to despise traditional villages and towns like 'the Garden City' or even the 'cité industrielle'. His anticipation was that big cities would double every 30 to 50 years. He believed that this was positive: urbanisation should continue unabated and even be encouraged until it became the 'natural state' for humans (Frisby 1997). Accordingly, his plan for Vienna was based on a network of ring roads and straight radial roads, which extended infinitely beyond the original Ringstrasse created in the mid-1800s. These roads were extra wide (80 to 100 metres) to accommodate all future traffic needs. Also, the secondary roads that enclosed the housing blocks were quite wide (23 metres). Unlike London, Wagner's Vienna would not be contained by a green belt (Geretsegger and Peintner 1970).

In this sense, Wagner's city was not child- or family-friendly. His drawings of streets often featured leisurely flâneurs, sometimes accompanied by elegant ladies. Wagner believed that the majority of city dwellers preferred anonymity in the crowd and emphasised the importance of grand urban spaces that allowed individuals to blend into the masses, rather than encouraging excessive social contact (Frisby 1997). Such anonymity could have served men well, as it allowed them more freedom to move around the city without social scrutiny. Did it provide women, especially middle-class women without established professions, with any level of independence?

Some commentators have argued that modern, anonymous urban spaces aided women's liberation by supporting their roles as shoppers, parkgoers, and strollers (Wilson 1992; Elkin 2017). However, non-working women were also at risk of becoming more isolated, lonely, and vulnerable in large cities, where they often lacked social connections and family support. Moreover, Wagner's optimistic assumption that all city dwellers already lived in a "modern" world could not have applied to women. In Austria, women did not obtain the right to vote until 1918, the year of Wagner's death.

While Wagner operated under a centralised and orderly empire, his planning ideas were not entirely undemocratic. A believer in 'municipal paternalism', he emphasised public land ownership and the distribution of urban resources to benefit all social classes and avoid the "vampire" of land speculation. Wagner's concern for a comprehensive and efficient rail system, including express services, reflected a desire to make the city accessible to a wide range of residents. He supported the creation of healthy and inexpensive rental housing in the form of mid-rise apartment buildings with simple, stern facades. Also, he insisted on providing each urban district with public amenities such as parks, playgrounds, schools, libraries, theatres, hospitals, department stores, police stations, and even morgues (Wagner 1912). While Wagner believed that art and aesthetics were essential in urban planning, he also cared a great deal about hygiene, order, and functionality. His motto was 'artis sola domina necessitas', meaning 'art knows only one master, need' (Frisby 1997).

Josef Stübben's struggle to balance tradition and modernity

Josef Stübben (1845–1936) was considered a key urban planning authority in his day. His theoretical work is still considered relevant for contemporary practice in his native Germany. By the time Stübben wrote his encyclopaedic book 'Urban Planning' ('Der Städtebau'), he already had considerable experience in the development of large projects in Germany and abroad. The first edition of his book was published in 1890, with revised editions appearing in 1907 and 1924. The final version stretched to more than 550 pages and included 900 illustrations of urban design solutions from existing cities in Europe. In addition to street and block patterns, the book covered myriad details, including tree grates, lawn edgings, and streetlamps (Figure 17).

Stübben's approach, like that of other German contemporaries, was to generate new planning ideas based on the systematic study of old urban structures (Cortjaens 2011). A close reading of his book reveals that the author was engaged in an inner struggle on how to strike a balance between 'tradition' and 'modernity'. On the one hand, he acknowledged Camillo Sitte's ideas

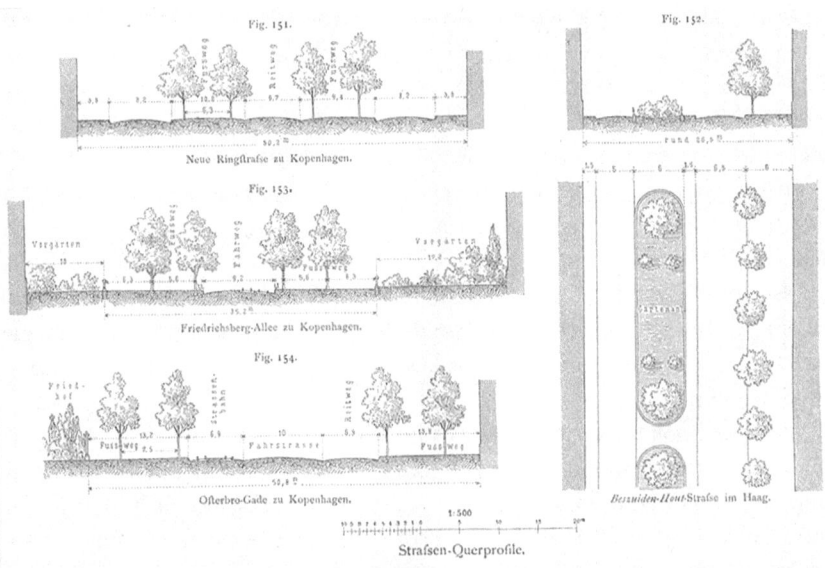

Figure 17 Street details in Stübben's book. Source: Wikimedia Commons. Image in the public domain.

hailing from neighbouring Vienna (which are discussed later in the book). For example, he praised the picturesque aspects of medieval cities and condemned the excessive clearance (disencumbering) around major monuments, such as cathedrals. He also lamented the pollution of waterfronts by factories, warehouses, and similar facilities (Stübben 2008[1907]).

On the other hand, Stübben was clearly captivated by Baron Haussmann's work in Paris and that city's advanced traffic engineering. He thought highly of Haussmann's ability to blend beauty and practicality by enhancing circulation while creating urban vistas and uniform street frontages (Ladd 1987). In the debate between the contained and historically grounded city as a work of art versus the formal, rational expansion of the city into a universal metropolis, he leaned towards the latter position (Frisby 2003). Not only the book, but also Stübben's 1881 plan for Cologne's Neustadt was a clear reflection of Haussmann's influence (Ladd 1987).[8]

Stübben believed in readable cities that facilitated the movement of people and goods – thereby supporting capitalism. Also, he emphasised the role of new technologies in urban development (Frisby 2003). He was among the first to propose a hierarchy of streets based on their transport function: through streets, diagonal streets, local streets, belt roads, and so on (Collins and Collins 1965). He was in favour of large metropoles that incorporated suburban growth into a coordinated whole, as opposed to the decentralised 'Garden City' models that were emerging in Great Britain at the time. Rather than designing whole towns as "gardens," he preferred the inclusion of parks within large cities. Like Frederick Law Olmsted (see page 60), Stübben believed that parks would not only provide spaces for children's play and adults' socialisation but also serve to counter urban "roughness," calm the mind, and educate youth in beauty and aesthetics.

In his physical design recommendations, Stübben sought to establish a middle ground in terms of building heights, road widths, and geometrical shapes. He was against both American-style skyscrapers and British-style single-family dwellings. He thought that conditions in continental Europe favoured cities populated by mid-rise multi-family homes. He condoned wide, straight streets as necessary in business districts but noted that these might become monotonous as well as unsanitary due to wind, dust, and lack of shade. The book advocated plans with visual variety, for example by including curved streets in city plans, especially in hilly terrain. Stübben believed that individualised urban spaces (streets, squares, parks, and neighbourhoods) were not necessarily the result of historic accident but could be planned as such.

Stübben supported private land and property rights and noted that landowners should be consulted before a plan approval. However, he was not a market libertarian. He stated that "legislation limiting the right to build is an absolute necessity" as well as a common practice in "all highly civilized lands." He also believed in eminent domain, that is, the right of planning authorities to expropriate private property for public benefit (upon compensation) (Stübben 2008[1907]). Moreover, Stübben criticised sharply the phenomenon of land and housing speculation in rapidly growing cities, which he saw as unethical to the point of "evil" as it created price bubbles, high rents, and overcrowding among the poor. He wrote that "the letting of workmen's dwellings is a disagreeable occupation. Well-meaning people therefore seldom invest money in such houses." The solution, according to Stübben, was non-profit housing construction by charities and the public sector. This planted the seed for the massive social housing programme that followed in Germany later in the twentieth century. (In-depth discussions of workers' housing and industrial zones are missing from the book.)

While a strong believer in regulation of markets and comprehensive planning, Stübben was hardly a revolutionary in the manner of his compatriot Karl Marx or Soviet architects like Nikolai Milyutin. He was a realist and a technocrat. Although he disapproved of physical segregation by social class, he did not seek to change the German social class structure nor do away with it altogether. Taking for granted that poverty would continue to exist in cities, he sought to improve the "piteous" and "wretched" housing conditions of impoverished workers but did so as a safeguard against criminality and immorality. Like many contemporaries in Europe and North America (see Baar 1992), he feared that a lack of sun, drainage, and ventilation would undermine family life, public security, and bourgeois morality:

> It is a well-known fact that the narrower and dingier the quarter of the city, the denser and more unattractive the dwellings, the more remote from bright sunshine and the freshness of nature – the rougher and coarser are the people, the wilder the boys and girls, the more neglected the children. [...] The swarms of children are obliged to play in the half-dark corridors, the narrow, high-walled courts and the streets. The parents can take no pleasure in their home; outside recreation, immorality, crime are the results. (Stübben 2008[1907])

On women's role in the city, he was entirely silent, and his views on workers' housing rights (presumably men) were often patronising. For example, he thought that homeownership was only appropriate for the leisurely upper and middle classes, whereas workers who purchased a house would not become "sound citizens" but rather end up being bound to a specific place or factory. While Stübben claimed to be primarily concerned about workers' welfare here, a footloose labour force also served the needs of capital. Additionally, Stübben feared that, as homeowners, workers may opt to rent out rooms, reintroducing issues like overcrowding.

While supportive of rental low-income housing, he was quite dogmatic in terms of its size and design, presuming to know workers' needs better than they knew themselves. This was typical of early planners. Stübben thought that, in most large cities, a working-class family needed just two or three rooms. More space would be disempowering, as workers lacked furniture for spare rooms, and the temptation to earn extra cash via subletting was too great. Subletting was, in fact, a major concern in that era.

Finally, Stübben wrote that in worker housing "a little garden [was] all the more unnecessary because a city workman would not know how to care for it" (Stübben 2008 [1907]). The possibility of women growing food for their families in those gardens had not occurred to him. In contrast, some of Stübben's contemporaries in the United States would have been delighted to see tenement dwellers partake in wholesome occupations such as gardening rather than "indulging unjustifiably in theatre-parties, fur cloaks, and automobiles" (cited in Baar 1992). Interestingly, the practice of urban farming in private gardens or public allotments became quite common in Europe during and immediately after World War II, and now this movement is trending once again.

Daniel Burnham's plan of Chicago and the City Beautiful

City planner and architect Daniel Burnham (1846–1912), in collaboration with fellow planner Edward Bennett and male leaders of the Chicago business community (Burnham and Bennett 1909), developed the 1909 Plan of Chicago. This plan is now considered one of the key documents of the City Beautiful movement, which emerged at the turn of the twentieth century in response to the rapid urbanisation and industrialisation sweeping across North America. The movement sought to counter the social problems of cities by promoting planning principles focused on aesthetics, order, and grandeur. Influenced by the City Beautiful ethos, many cities undertook ambitious projects to reshape their spaces via monumental civic plazas, scenic parks, and grand boulevards. Although its influence waned by World War II, the City Beautiful movement left an indelible mark on a range of US cities.

When he was commissioned to prepare the plan of Chicago, Burnham had prior experience working on master plans for Washington, D.C., Cleveland, and San Francisco. Additionally, he had been responsible for leading the design of Chicago's monumental architecture for the highly successful 1893

World's Columbian Exposition, which attracted many tourists to the rapidly growing industrial centre. However, unpaved roads, poor sanitation, overcrowding, and smoke pollution made the cityscape dirty and unhealthy. Movement of people and freight was restricted and slow in central areas, and large railway yards separated the commercial centre and parts of the city south of the river from the lakefront. Impacted by the depression and the 1894 workers' strike at Pullman, the social setting in late 1890s Chicago was also challenging. Industrial working conditions were poor, and the city suffered from high rates of homelessness, hunger, and infant mortality.

Burnham stated that the 1909 plan was based on the "careful study of the needs of Chicago, made by disinterested men of wide experience" (Burnham and Bennett 1909: 2). However, the plan did not seek to address social conditions or the housing crisis. Rather, it prioritised urban beautification and transport infrastructure works (Figure 18), as a tool to attract investment and respond to commercial and tourism interests (Flanagan 2018). In preparing the plan, Burnham drew on historical precedents of large urban centres (international and national). His plan had six main areas of focus: (1) Lakefront improvements, including extensive public parklands and harbour facilities; (2) Outer parks created through the public acquisition of natural areas; (3) New cultural and civic centres; (4) Regional highways in radial lines connecting the centre to the hinterland and also circumnavigating the urban area; (5) Major arterial roads and boulevards leading out from the city centre and the addition of a network of diagonal streets; and (6) Railway terminal consolidation and development of an integrated track system for passengers and commercial freight (Smith 2006). Many of Chicago's housing issues were intractable, as they were entwined with prejudice and the segregation of residents based on race and class. African American residents were concentrated on the south side in overcrowded and substandard accommodation (Flanagan 2018).

Gender was also an issue. Burnham prioritised a narrowly defined public interest – specifically one concerned with economic development through the protection of private property and the commercial or industrial wealth interests of a few prominent businessmen. Women were excluded from the consultation and design process, notwithstanding their activism. Women's 'street-level' understanding of the city as a place of belonging was dismissed as irrelevant. Ongoing requests by women to have public toilets for women and children included in major civic buildings, parks, and street widening projects fell on deaf ears. Similarly, women's requests for children's playgrounds in residential neighbourhoods and along the lakeside parklands were ignored, as were their demands for plans to address housing (Flanagan 2018):

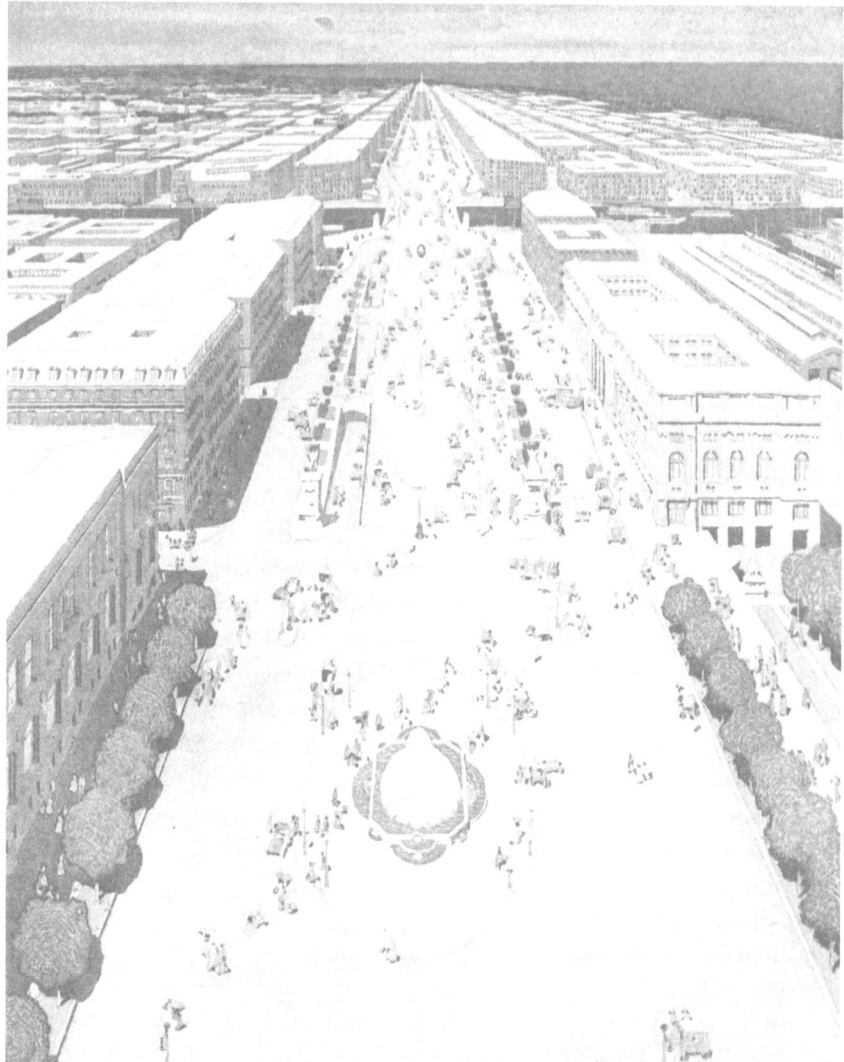

Figure 18 Proposed design for Chicago, view looking north from Washington Street. Source: Plan of Chicago. Image in the public domain.

Men and women in […] Chicago both used the phrase *City of Homes* to refer to the city, but men meant single-family home ownership, and women meant that the city was a home for all its residents. […] One Chicago newspaper even castigated women for wanting to live in apartments rather than buying homes Flanagan. (2018: 70)

This approach only served to reinforce patriarchal power structures and cement single-home ownership as the preferred urban housing option in the United States. Ignoring the input of women in the replanning process, Burnham's 1909 Plan for Chicago effectively segregated men and women by creating an urban environment that was designed by and for men. Similarly, disregarding the chronically dismal housing conditions of the masses, and prioritising the spatial separation of public activities from private ones, created and reinforced gendered roles (Flanagan 2018).

Patrick Geddes and the advent of biological ideas in planning

Patrick Geddes (1854–1932) was a Scottish biologist and planner. He produced a series of canonical texts, including *Cities in Evolution* (1949 [1915]), concerned with locating cities within a regional context and presenting a socioecological understanding of urbanisation. Geddes was interested in the connections between spatial form and social processes, focusing on the co-dependency of healthy ecosystems and social systems. He stressed the importance of access to the countryside and nature for women and children's health:

> The children, the women, the workers of the town come but rarely to the country. As hygienists, and utilitarians, we must therefore bring the country to them. (Geddes 1949 [1915]: 14,52,68)

Out of concern for women's health, he advocated for height restrictions on apartments:

> There is a distinct stratum of women's ill health, and with this children's also, on the fourth storey, and of course upwards? Why? Because while a woman will contentedly go up and down one stair or two, or even three, the fourth is the last straw, and when carrying a basket on one arm and a baby on the other a very substantial one. She is [...] [in the] habit of going out as little as possible, which of course opens the way to a new series of ailments. (Geddes (1949 [1915]): 68,69)

He articulated the expansion and design of British cities using biological principles drawn from Darwin's theory of evolution. He postulated that human societies, cultures, and races, like natural organisms, can and do evolve and progress over time. Unlike some of his contemporaries who emphasised biological determinism, Geddes placed more importance on cultural and environmental factors – including topography and climate – in shaping human societies. One of his key contributions was the 'valley section', a conceptual model that illustrated the relationship between geography, human settlements, and economic activities along a natural gradient from the mountains

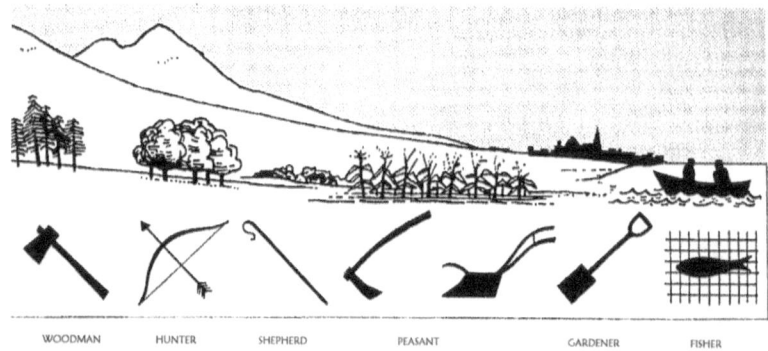

Figure 19 Valley section. Source: Wikimedia Commons. Image in the public domain.

to the sea (Figure 19). This model highlighted how different ecological zones support different types of activities and conglomerations.

In some ways, his early ideas aligned with contemporary ecofeminist concerns about sustainability, social justice, sprawl, loss of biodiversity, resource availability, and the resilience of people and environments in urban settings. Modern bioregionalism, a concept emphasising the importance of living within the natural characteristics and constraints of a region, draws significant inspiration from Geddes's ideas. Like today's bioregionalists, he supported the idea of localism, believing that local communities should have control over their development and that solutions should be tailored to local conditions.

However, Geddes's ideas were also shaped by the colonial context of his time. While he was critical of some aspects of colonialism, his views on race and culture were paternalistic at times, reflecting the prevailing attitudes of Western superiority and pseudo-scientific ideas of race. With regard to gender, Geddes, like other men of his time, was an essentialist and advocated the concept of the Two Spheres: men in public affairs and women in the private domain of home and family (Meller 1990). Presumably rooted in human biology, this model imposed a sexual division of labour. Geddes believed women's innately nurturing nature was essential for humanising cities affected by modern capitalism, finance, and industry (Meller 1990: 88). He argued that women's roles were complementary to men's and crucial for social reform, as women – untainted by the corrupting influences of the public world – transmitted positive values to future generations (Flanagan 2018).

John Nolen's merging of nature and urbanism

John Nolen (1868–1937) is considered as a founder of the modern city planning movement in the United States. Having studied landscape architecture with Frederick Law Olmsted (see page 60), Nolen sought to merge urbanism and nature in a socially meaningful way. Like Olmsted, he believed that access to nature could address the physical and moral health of citizens and boost their happiness. His inspiration came from European urban reforms, especially in Germany, and the English Garden City movement, spearheaded by Raymond Unwin (see page 65). Nolen's practice was prolific. In his lifetime, he completed over 400 projects, 29 city plans, and 27 new town plans (Stephenson 2015a), and played key roles in early professional planning organisations which promoted the use of planning experts by governments. His designs were underpinned by strong philosophical and economic principles which he promoted through his writing, including the book *New Ideals in the Planning of Cities, Towns and Villages* (1919).

While being reform-minded, Nolen was not a radical. He wished to respond to commercial interests while also addressing the socio-technical problems associated with rapid urbanisation. A clear communicator, he directly appealed to the financial aspirations of state and local governments and Chambers of Commerce. He strongly encouraged the establishment of surveying and planning departments tasked with the comprehensive analysis of the natural, social, and economic conditions of cities and towns, and supported the appointment of planning commissioners responsible for the ongoing implementation of masterplans. A belief that a comprehensive and future-focused approach to planning could improve the well-being of all individuals underpinned Nolen's work. He wrote: "We need to make improvements for the benefit and enjoyment of everybody, for the common good" (Nolen 1919: 17.)

Nolen understood the importance of setting out an interconnected and rational system of streets to establish city plans and contain urban spread. He used the natural topography to inform his designs, seeking to preserve existing tracts of nature. His grid layouts were punctuated by public parks at more or less regular intervals to ensure near-universal access to greenery. Public open space was also created along foreshores and watercourses (Figure 20). Nolen's wide, tree-lined main streets supported vehicles but also pedestrians; peripheral residential areas had more naturalised and curved streets (Stephenson 2015a). In terms of physical planning, this approach was superior to what had been available earlier. Grounded in the American reality of the early twentieth century, the cities and neighbourhoods that Nolen envisioned were also more liveable and sustainable than the outlandish urban spaces imagined by his compatriot and contemporary, Frank Lloyd Wright (see page 15) or, across the ocean, Le Corbusier (see page 23). In fact, Nolenian-style urbanism was a major inspiration for the New Urbanist movement of the 1980s.

Figure 20 Perspective sketch of the San Diego bayfront, showing the Paseo connecting the bay with the city park. Source: John Nolen and Geo. H. Ellis Co. Image in the public domain.

In other ways, Nolan's approach to urban planning reflected that of his Western male peers in the emerging planning profession, as well as commonly held distinctions about class, gender, and race. He actively applied hierarchical zoning in his plans: commercial and public buildings and spaces were usually grouped in a linear fashion in city centres, exclusively residential areas circled the centre, and industrial and production activities were placed on the urban fringe. Topographical features and vegetation screens were used to compartmentalise plan areas by function and social class. Similar controls applied to residential dwelling types and heights, with dwellings for the wealthier located in more central locations, and poorer residents on the city edges (Beck 2009).

In this manner, Nolen enabled a distinction between public and private life in cities and towns (Stephenson 2015b). His plans ultimately resulted in a built environment that prioritised the needs of white, mobile, healthy, and employable men. While residential zones included enclaves that could potentially address the unmet shelter needs of men and women of colour (Stephenson 2015b), the detached private family home was a cornerstone of Nolen's designs:

> Nolen was strongly committed to the detached single-family house as the ideal form of residence – though his broader political commitment to a society and metropolis segregated by occupation, class and race does not necessarily require the dominance of this particular residential ideal. [...] Nolen's ideal metropolitan landscape was ordered at the large scale by a belief in the arrangement of landscapes by function and demographic groups and at the more immediate scale of the street

and residential lot by a belief in private family residences which were clearly distinct both by their separation from each other and by their regimentation along the street through the use of uniform front and side setbacks. (Beck 2009: 99,102)

While the cities that Nolen himself planned were relatively small, in larger settlements, zoning, coupled with a predominance of single-family housing, created large distances between residential areas and centres of commerce, education, work, recreation, and education. This produced inequalities in terms of access. The creation of homogenous neighbourhoods and racially segregated cities was not necessarily an accident. At the turn of the twentieth century, purchases of automobiles and single-family homes were beyond the budgets of most single women and people of colour. Nolen may have made some very deliberate planning and landscaping choices to appease the city leaders with whom he worked and "heighten the symbolic order of the centres of power in the city" (Beck 2009: 33). Compartmentalisation is now a standard feature of North American cities.

Patrick Abercrombie's professionalised planning process

Originally trained as an architect, Patrick Abercrombie (1879–1957) built a long and internationally distinguished academic and professional career as a planner. In Britain, he was a leading advocate for the state administration and professionalisation of the urban planning movement. In 1909, he became editor of the newly established *Town Planning Review* and was a founding member of the Town Planning Institute (Hall 1995; Dehaene 2004). As an academic, he held key roles at the University of Liverpool and University College London. Overall, he played a key role in establishing the model of the professional planner.

Expanding his focus beyond housing and suburbs, Abercrombie prioritised understanding places within the context of their regional setting and function – advocating for the preservation of nature and the countryside. He generated just under twenty regional plans in the interwar period (Amati and Freestone 2009; Figure 21) but became best known for his plan for London, prepared at the end of World War II (White 2019). In these plans, much like his contemporaries, Abercrombie assigned a low priority to women's needs in cities. This is evidenced, for example, in his 1914 competition-winning plan for Dublin, which sought to support the anticipated growth of shipping and industry in the city. The plan envisioned the widening of existing streets in established neighbourhoods, effectively displacing thousands of residents and demolishing a centrally located maternity hospital (Flanagan 2013).

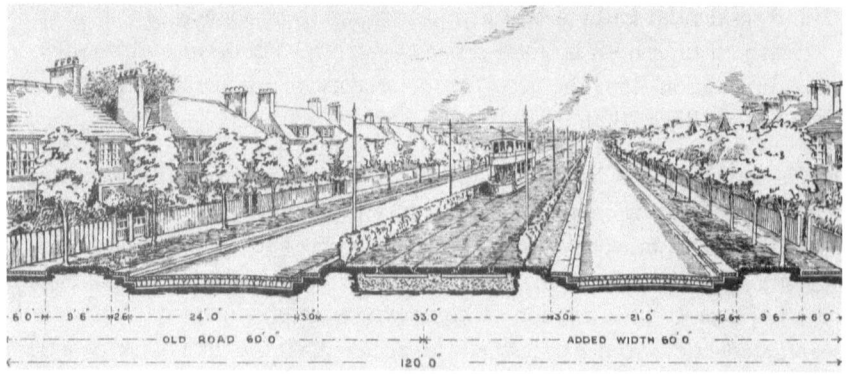

Figure 21 Road widening project in Liverpool. Source: Liverpool Town Planning and Housing Exhibition. Image in the public domain.

Abercrombie published his leading book, *Town and Country Planning* in 1933 (Abercrombie and Childs 1959[1933]). Drawing on international precedents, he presented a history and theory of planning and promoted a model for the practice of planning. He argued for the conservation of the English countryside and the preservation of distinct but complementary areas of city and country in a region. In addition, he discussed the importance of replanning existing city centres and improving civic architecture through a staged process. In terms of housing, Abercrombie advocated for slum clearance and replacement with new tenements (instead of single-family homes). However, his main concern was with reducing traffic congestion in city centres. He listed his priorities as follows:

> the management of traffic away from shopping and business areas; rationalisation of traffic in the city centre; centralisation of administrative functions'; connection of shopping streets; the creation of new streets "through worn out property"; greater connectivity between railway stations; the creation of parking space near city centres. (Abercrombie and Childs 1959[1933]: 151–166)

This approach did not make British cities family- or child-friendly – although Abercrombie did advocate strongly for the creation and preservation of open space in his city replanning:

> for children under 14 there should be ½ acre which should be distributed that no child should have to walk more than ¼ mile to reach a play space. (Abercrombie and Childs 1959[1933]: 148)

Beyond this quote, women and children were rarely mentioned in the text. This absence is not just a quirk of language. In the book, Abercrombie clearly defined the role of planning as supporting an adult male workforce:

> Town planning, in a word, intends to make the city in every way a more convenient place to work in, aiming at designing and remodelling its business quarters, manufacturing districts, railway facilities and waterfront, so as to save money to the business man and allow the citizen to go to and from his work with the least loss of time and energy. (Abercrombie and Childs 1959[1933]: 109)

Abercrombie expanded on Patrick Geddes' three-step process to planning: survey of existing conditions, data analysis, and then plan preparation. In the second part of the book, he described the value of understanding a locality in the development of a plan for that locality. In fact, Abercrombie became highly regarded for his survey work (Hall 1995). However, both Geddes's and Abercrombie's methods were inadequate from a feminist perspective:

> Geddes's management of the civic survey was as gendered as his concept of women's role in the city. He sent both teams of male and female students to survey city neighbourhoods, but gender determined their task. Men were to report on the quality of housing; women were "to record anything they thought interesting" to "learn about social engagement". [...] When Abercrombie enthusiastically embraced the concept of the survey, he turned it into a professional tool and removed women totally from participating in surveying the city. (Flanagan 2018: 123)

With hindsight, Abercrombie's approach set a precedent for a patriarchal model of planning, which promoted professional methods that excluded women's everyday realities while prioritising economic growth and the movement of male workers and goods through cities at the expense of existing residential neighbourhoods.

The Romantic Archaists

In contrast to the rational functionalists, who were future-oriented, the romantic archaists were anti-modernists. Drawn to history, tradition, and the symbolic richness of past civilisations, they sought to preserve what they saw as the moral and aesthetic values of earlier times. They advocated for a more organic, emotionally resonant approach to urban design, fearing that technological progress would erode human connection and meaning.

Frederick Law Olmsted's urban parks and garden suburbs

Frederick Law Olmsted (1822–1903) was an American landscape architect, city planner, writer, and agriculturist. He lived at a time when the provision of large urban parks came to be seen as a solution to the health and morality problems caused by urbanisation and industrialisation, as well as an equalising and civilising factor for the working classes. Physical exercise, social interaction, order, and mental and visual respite could be achieved by accessing and appreciating green and picturesque landscapes. Olmsted was, in fact, a major contributor to this planning philosophy (Scheper 1989). While he also produced regional and urban plans, he is best known for his work on the design and engineering of large naturalistic landscapes in urban settings, including the garden suburb of Riverside in Illinois, Central Park in Manhattan, and Prospect Park in Brooklyn, New York.

Central Park and Prospect Park were strategically designed to be realised over time and sequentially experienced predominately on foot. Pastoral and picturesque aesthetics dominated, reflecting rural scenery with soft indistinct boundaries, large green open spaces, rolling grasslands, lakes, rocks, shrubs, and trees sited to screen and contrast deliberately with the hard edges of gridiron city planning. A residential suburb, Riverside, was also designed to resemble a park (Figure 22). Housing lots were connected by curved and tree-lined transportation corridors. These supported pedestrian access but also eased vehicle movement.

A socially connected man, Olmsted was well-read and well-travelled. Visiting Liverpool in 1850, he was impressed and inspired by Birkenhead – the first public park in England – which appeared to be used by men, women, and children from all walks of life. He observed:

> I was glad to observe that the privileges of the garden were enjoyed about equally by all classes. There were some who were attended by servants, and sent at once for their carriages, but a large proportion were of the common ranks, and a few women with children, or suffering from ill health, were evidently the wives of very humble labourers.
> (Olmstead 1922: 97)

Olmsted's advocacy for egalitarian public access to green space and nature through large urban parks has been considered by some commentators as "democratic, reformist, and indeed, feminist" (Scheper 1989: 369). Others have noted that existing ideas about race and class underpinned Olmsted's belief that designing suburban landscapes and public parks to maximise their natural beauty could improve the moral, social, and spiritual standing of users:

ANALYSIS

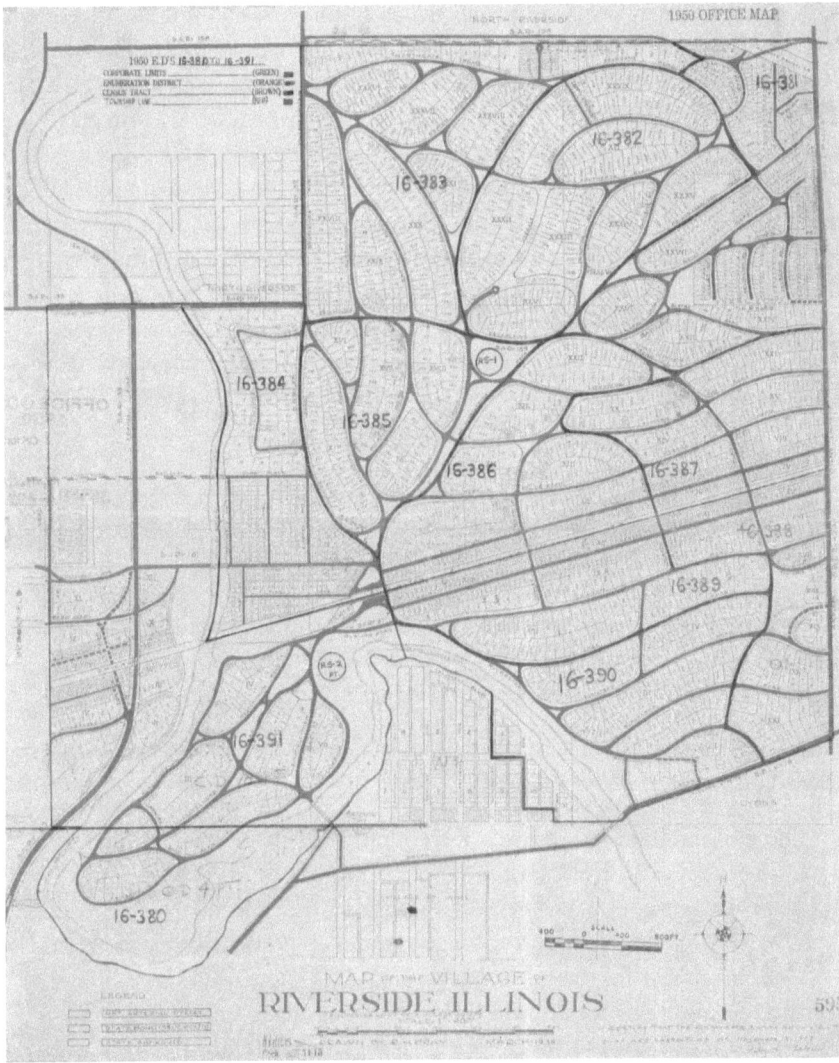

Figure 22 Riverside layout, as it appeared in 1950. Source: US National Archives and Records Administration. Image in the public domain.

This point of view privileged a single experience – the contemplation of the landscape – over the demands of working-class and immigrant groups for more active and varied recreation, such as competitive sports and popular entertainments, which Olmstead banished from Central Park. (Crawford 1995: 64)

While migrant workers' needs and wants were marginalised, "respectable" women were expected to perform a key role in the reform agenda associated with the creation of urban parks. At this time, the family unit was seen as an antidote to growing civic unrest. Urban society depended on women to act as a moral compass and quell men's undesirable habits and urges, including laziness, alcoholism, delinquency, and solicitation of prostitution. While middle-class women were generally constrained in their outdoor movements, spending time in a park was considered healthy and decorous. Similarly, men displaying a wife and children in a safe public setting like a park projected stability and virtue. Therefore, making parks attractive to families – especially women and the children they were supervising – was an important criterion for landscape designers (Cranz 1980). To this professional principle, Olmsted added a personal and somewhat sentimental motive:

> My mother died while I was so young that I have but a tradition of memory rather than the faintest recollection of her. While I was a small schoolboy if I was asked if I remembered her I could say "Yes; I remember playing on the grass and looking up at her while she sat sewing under a tree." I now only remember that I did so remember her, but it has always been a delight to me to see a woman sitting under a tree, sewing and minding a child. (Olmstead 1922: 46)

However, for this idyllic image to materialise in Central Park, a thriving Black community was destroyed:

> The city had cleared the way for its hallowed park by evicting 1,600 or so people who lived on the land. Among those displaced were the residents of Seneca Village, Manhattan's first significant settlement of black property owners and the epicenter of black political power in Manhattan during the mid-19th century. [...] Nevertheless, real estate interests and their minions in the press set the stage for what the writer James Baldwin would later describe as "Negro removal" by defaming the flourishing enclave as a "shantytown" and a "nigger village". (Staples 2019)

Camillo Sitte and city planning as an artistic endeavour

A Viennese architect and artist, Camillo Sitte (1843–1903), published his highly influential planning book *The Art of Building Cities* in 1889, well before he had personally designed a city plan. His work in provincial towns throughout the Hapsburg Empire followed later, once the book became well known in the German-speaking community and beyond, and Sitte's maverick reputation was established (Hanisch 2010). The book took the planning world by storm. While most of his contemporaries praised rational planning (meaning straight streets, square plazas, star-shaped roundabouts, and uniform setbacks), Sitte scorned geometrical exactitude, which, he charged, was devastating historic districts and producing banal urban extensions. To Sitte, the primacy of engineering considerations such as efficiency of traffic flow (above-ground) or ease of plumbing installations (underground) was untenable (Collins and Collins 1965). He even charged that San Francisco's regular grid, mindlessly imposed on a hilly and windy terrain, was hideous (Sitte 1945[1889]).

As the book's title indicates, Sitte favoured the picturesque and organic character of European, particularly Italian, cities and towns that had survived the industrialisation era, be they Greco-Roman, Medieval, Renaissance, or Baroque (Sitte 1945[1889]). From the examples of those cities, which he had visited, Sitte extracted a series of principles by which he critiqued contemporaneous planning and proposed solutions to restore the artistic basis of the planning profession – in Vienna and farther afield (Collins and Collins 1965). His visual analysis was a major contribution to urban history, although the book pointedly addressed planners rather than historians (Hanisch 2010). The tone was polemic, and some of the leading planners of the day, particularly Reinhard Baumeister, were regularly called out (Sitte 1945[1889]).

Sitte's book highlighted the charm of irregular setbacks, protruding elements, interrupted views, limited panoramas, and "crooked" streets (Cortjaens 2011; Figure 23). While he never proposed a comprehensive plan or vision for Vienna, he maintained that a city should be regarded as a total work of art rather than the mere sum of its parts. Even tree planting should fit into the urban rhythms and patterns rather than follow neat rows along the streets. Sitte's proposed approach to planning resembled the curation of a three-dimensional exhibition. To him, the result would not simply bring aesthetic pleasure but it would make humans feel secure and happy and cure modern anomie.

While his colleagues concentrated on fighting infectious diseases resulting from overcrowding and poor sanitation, Sitte was among the few to show sensitivity to psychological well-being. This element of care is symbolically more feminine than the obsession with utilitarian matters that prevailed in his day. Interestingly, Sitte insisted that public squares should be as enclosed, attractive, and intimate as the interior spaces of the (bourgeois) home – which were associated with the female gender – in order to function well as civic spaces (Frisby 2003). In later decades, the revitalisation of public spaces in conjunction with the public sphere (and democracy itself) became central to the progressive political agenda (Sonne 2009).

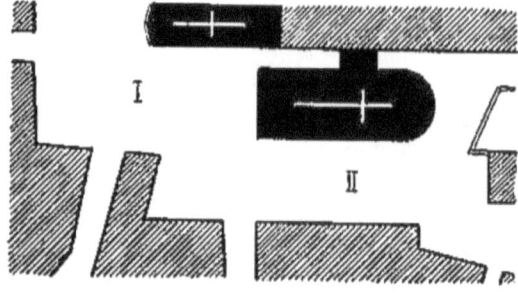

REGENSBURG:
I. Domplatz.   II. Domstraße.

Figure 23 Typical illustration in Sitte's book. Source: Wikimedia Commons. Image in the public domain.

Sitte's book spoke to all urban dwellers, rather than singling out and patronising the working classes, as others had done. In this, he was a humanist. His yearning for human scale in city-making is another humanistic aspect of Sitte's work (Collins and Collins 1965). He appreciated the collective, piecemeal city-making efforts of the past – a process which radically differed from the comprehensive plans produced in one stroke by individual men in the nineteenth century (Frisby 2003).

Many commentators have given Sitte major credit for rekindling the artistic consciousness of the planning profession (Ladd 1987) and even dubbed him the "father of modern planning." However, his aesthetic, apolitical focus has also been the target of critics (Hanisch 2010). Sitte has been accused of elitism (Ladd 1987), and some have questioned whether one can plan cities without considering social aspects such as poverty, unemployment, deprivation, and marginalisation (by race, gender, and so on). Some have also noted that Sitte's picturesque ideal can be read as lending support to small-scale, essentially conservative urban ensembles, predicated on the decentralisation of political power (Moravánszky 2006). A group of Sitte's followers in Germany even linked the concept of picturesque Garden Cities with nationalist and racist intentions – presumably to contrast the internationalist ethos of left-wing politics (Sonne 2009).

However, Sitte was not naïve; nor was he a Luddite or a bigot (Hanisch 2010). In the book, he acknowledged the technical achievements of his era and openly admitted that society had reached a point of no return. Mechanisation could not be undone. While he insisted that the artistic potential of each urban site be explored, some of his recommendations towards the end of the book resembled those of his peers. He even went as far as mentioning feasibility studies and statistical analyses (Sitte 1945[1889]). It was a surrender of sorts. The "accidents of history" he so loved in Florence and Venice could not be recreated ex-novo in planned cities. Should someone try, the result would appear contrived (Moravánszky 2006). In fact, Sitte did not have much respect for the faux-picturesque garden suburbs en vogue in the United States. In his hometown of Vienna, he was particularly unhappy with the Ringstrasse project,[9] which created sterile self-standing monuments surrounded by open space. However, he did praise Haussmann and the version of Paris the baron created (Sitte 1945[1889]). This indicates that Sitte was a sophisticated thinker who understood that in the modern world, any effort to elevate the authority of the artist above all else would be quixotic.

Raymond Unwin and the return to picturesque village life

Raymond Unwin (1863–1940) was a British architect and planner, as well as a key figure in the 'Garden City' movement. In 1909, he wrote *Town Planning in Practice*, a highly influential text that was repeatedly republished (Unwin 1994[1909]). This work provided directions on the design of new neighbourhoods and towns. Parts of the book were clearly influenced by Ebenezer Howard's and Camillo Sitte's planning ideas (see pages 12 and 62). Practical applications of the principles promoted by Unwin are found in the 'Garden Cities' of Letchworth, Hampstead, and Welwyn in England and Yorkship and Mariemont in the United States, all of which were built in the early twentieth century (Figure 24). Unwin was directly responsible for Letchworth's planning,[10] which is often considered as the first realised Garden City. Architecturally, he was partial to the Arts and Crafts movement.

Unwin's views were typically middle-class. He was content with indirect means of social reform – for example, by remodelling the built environment. He strongly advocated for a return to picturesque village life and praised the advantages of this lifestyle over urban living. Unwin's ideal density was fairly low: twelve detached or semi-detached homes per acre. He saw the sparsely populated village as a social stabiliser that could support community life and familial bonds, ensure social-democratic equality, and allow for Christian compassion.

Unwin's nostalgic image of the cottage was emblematic of the healthy and upstanding middle-class family (Crawford 1995; Creese 1994). He proposed that cottage interiors be specifically designed to foster domesticity. They were to contain a large communal room in which:

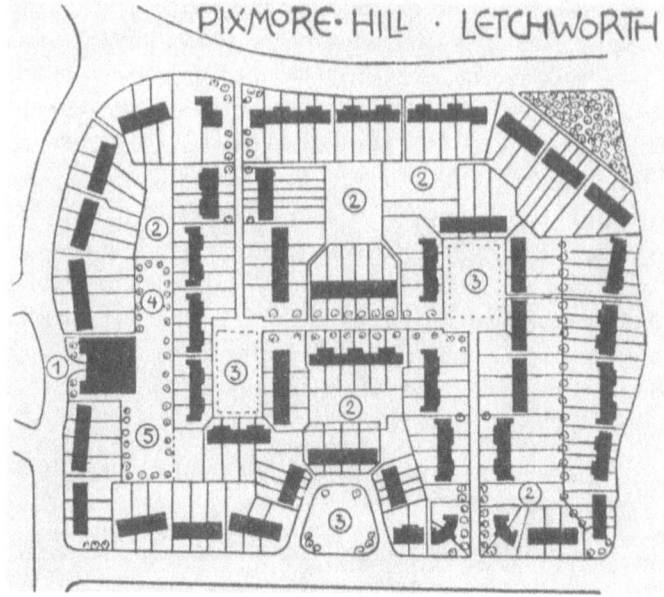

Figure 24 Plan for Letchworth. Source: Wikimedia Commons. Image in the public domain.

> the bulk of the domestic work will be done, meals will be prepared and eaten, and children will play, while the whole family will often spend long evenings there together. (Unwin 1994[1909]: 67)

This layout would have women embounded into that room and into 'quadrangles' – that is, outside spaces enclosed by fences or walls. Quads would replace the open backyards of earlier eras where women were not under surveillance. Such designs revealed no sense that all genders could or should belong to a democratic city (Flanagan 2013). Meanwhile, in laying out principles for the design of city centres and public spaces, Unwin's imagined subject was the male suburban commuter (Flanagan 2018):

> To secure that they shall be genuine centres where people will be likely to congregate, they must either be themselves the focal points of the main traffic lines, or must lie very near to these points, the latter in many ways being preferable. (Unwin 1994[1909]: 187)

SYNTHESIS

Having analysed each planner's work separately, we now synthesise the main themes that characterise this collective body of work as masculinist. Our synthesis is placed in the context of the urban history unfolding during the Second Industrial Revolution, as presented by contemporary feminist scholars. Additionally, we discuss the preoccupations of female planners, architects, and social reformers who were active in that era. As we explain, their focus was distinct from that of their male peers.

Central Themes in Masculine Early Utopias

Rigid form and triumphal scale. A reverence for geometry, order, and standardisation, which emerged during the Second Industrial Revolution, reflected a hegemonic and monolithic vision of the city, with low tolerance for cultural and physical difference (Frisby 2003). This goes against social-anarcha-feminist tenets of co-design and communal decision-making. With male planners at the helm, the city became a series of discrete objects instead of an "ensemble of relations" (Frisby 2003).

While some thinkers protested this approach, most early planning treatises can be understood as a masculine fantasy of control – of space, time, women, race, and the rest of life (Hooper 1998; Johns 2010). Unsurprisingly, during that era, romantic notions of place and time came to be associated with female sentimentality (Flanagan 2018). Even Howard and Unwin, who advocated for human-scale settlements, did so in a paternalistic manner. Planners who emerged from the architecture profession, such as Sitte and Taut, were overly concerned with physical form, neglecting other aspects such as health, the economy, or the environment.

Whether they were imagining utopias or intervening in existing settlements, most early planners envisioned the built-up spaces within cities and the natural landscapes surrounding cities as a blank slate, containing little historical memory or ecological value. Planning was used to decontextualise and instrumentalise those spaces to suit the abstract needs of the market

(Frisby 2003) or the state. Limitless urban growth and rapid, effortless speed of movement came to be valorised. While building heights were constrained in nineteenth-century plans by the lack of elevators, the sky became the new limit in the early twentieth century. Also, for the first time in history, roads became more important than houses (Marcus 2001). A focus on urban expansion is dialectically opposed to ecofeminist notions of de-growth.

The urban design drawings from that era contained humans and buildings but were also increasingly populated by instruments and machines – Le Corbusier's aerodromes, Sant'Elia's generators, Garnier's furnaces. In their eeriness and unfamiliarity, they represented the future, progress, and modernity (Hooper 2002). Unlike the agrarian utopians of the First Industrial Revolution, who idealised rural life and nature, utopian planners that came of age during the Second Industrial Revolution were often enamoured of technology (Markus 2003). Perhaps they were the precursors of Silicon Valley's "tech bros."

It is no coincidence that socio-spatial pathologies such as agoraphobia, amnesia, neurasthenia, monomania, and so on, made their appearance in the late nineteenth century (Frisby 2003). A strong need for safe and rigid order (as experienced in one's childhood) can even be interpreted as neuroticism and immaturity on the planners' part (Markus 2003). Ironically, the emergence of new disciplines such as sociology and public hygiene was crucial in allowing male reformers to present their ideas and defend their own pathologies as rational and scientific (Flanagan 2018). Some critics (e.g. Frisby 2003) have argued that an obsession with Euclidean form was ableist, in addition to being sexist: in the thinking of planners ranging from Haussmann to Wright, features such as the straight line and the megalomanic scale negate and even violate the human body in all its shapes, colours, ailments, and pain (Frisby 2003).

Spatial segregation by gender, class, and race. Many of those same planners who lacked interest in cultural and physical differences readily accepted that class differences would continue to endure in cities. Large-scale comprehensive plans, such as Le Corbusier's utopian Cité Radieuse or Daniel Burnham's Plan of Chicago, were certainly hierarchical: their physical designs were underpinned by concentric social schemes, with the wealthiest or most powerful occupying the seat of power at the centre (Markus 2003). But so were the plans for smaller settlements.

In Pullman's mill town, different workers were assigned different quality housing based on their skill level, whereas Olmsted's garden suburb of Riverside was designed to be attractive to middle- and upper-middle-class families. The concept of "slums" did not exist before the Second Industrial Revolution, nor did ideas around the "worthy poor" (i.e. the respectable members of the working class as opposed to the criminal and immoral lower classes). Slum housing was not conceptualised as organic and mutable but reduced to an object containing social ills to be cured via spatial reordering (Flanagan 2018; Frisby 2003).

The Second Industrial Revolution and resulting pollution necessitated the separation of industrial sectors from the rest of the city, particularly residential neighbourhoods. Eventually, commercial districts were separated as well – particularly in North America. The effect of this functional segregation, which later came to be known as "zoning," spatially enforced divisions between the public (male) and private (female) spheres. Planners symbolically separated the sacred and profane, the disorderly from the orderly, the clean from the unclean, the healthy from the diseased (Greed 1994).

Women – especially those who did not fit the bourgeois mould, such as street vendors or sex workers – were seen as a significant cause of urban profanity, disorder, filth, and disease (Hooper 2003). Women of colour were consigned to the realm of domestic servitude. In a sense, zoning was a moral rather than a practical exercise (Greed 1994). By and large, male planners, architects, and engineers – aided by other professionals such as doctors – manifested a quasi-religious zeal in their zoning work. But unlike earlier eras, their ideas were dressed in humanistic and scientific garb, whereas actual religion came to be associated with female irrationality and superstition (Greed 1994).

Idealisation of domesticity. Even as the planning agenda prioritised "men's issues" related to industry and commerce, domestic ideology was also promoted during this time (Flanagan 2018). In reality, many women in that era – ranging from factory workers and department store clerks to servants and prostitutes, not to mention female shoppers and museum visitors – were venturing out of the home (Sewell 2022; Elkin 2017). They could travel around the city on the new public transport systems being built from Madrid to Moscow – albeit those systems prioritised working men's commutes rather than women's 'mobilities of care'. However, women's movements were monitored in the vast and visible public spaces produced by male power (Hooper 1998; Flanagan 2018; Markus 2003; Wilson 1992). One simple but quite effective way to restrict women's mobility was men's refusal to build gender-segregated public toilets (Greed 1994; Flanagan 2018). Even the hyper-detailed urban design plates by Stübben and Alphand did not contain such facilities.

Thus, new planning schemes pushed middle- and upper-class women into the confines of the home – now increasingly built in urban peripheries as well as in city centres. (The plans by Milyutin and Soria y Mata were specifically meant as urban extensions.) In this isolated domestic realm, women were expected to cook, clean, and raise children (or preside over servants hired to complete those tasks) but not engage in paid labour. This setup was presented as liberating women from the toil of factory or office work (Markus 2003; Mozingo 2011). But the real purpose was to provide the tranquillity and stability that working men needed at the end of the day (Flanagan 2018).

The new concept of the "angel in the house" – like the contemporary 'tradwife'[1] – embodied the ideal of the perfect woman: a loyal and obedient wife and mother, passive and powerless but also graceful, selfless, and pure. This discourse was necessary because cities – then as now – did not often provide adequate facilities for home-, child-, and elderly-care. Meanwhile, working women were portrayed as temptresses who caused the problem of urban overpopulation because of their low morals (Greed 1994). Social reformers such as Geddes and Howard were not unlike other men of that era: they believed that feminine nurturing qualities enhanced and "softened" urban life, but only if the city was restructured according to masculine ideals (Flanagan 2018).

Meanwhile, housework problems were not resolved during the Second Industrial Revolution. Despite technological advancements, women (as wives, daughters, and servants) were tremendously burdened by domestic drudgery as middle-class houses became increasingly ornate and working-class housing became overcrowded and derelict. A "domestic science movement" emerged to reduce women's workload but soon became another tool of social control in the hands of male inventors and engineers (Greed 1994). Interestingly, pre-industrial lifestyles and planning practices had not accommodated such judgements and divisions. A mixture of uses, even within the same building, had allowed women to more easily combine production, consumption, chores, and childrearing (Cherry 1979).

Some commentators have suggested that early planners in capitalist settings marginalised women and imprisoned them in suburbia because their true aim was not to serve humans but to clear out the city and subsequently shape it in the interest of capitalist production and consumption (Frisby 2003). Yet, women who lived in socialist towns, such as the one proposed by Milyutin or the ones implemented in North America (Hayden 1976), did not fare much better. Here, women were treated as "comrades" on one level. But, on another level, they were treated as collective property to be shared and used by men according to their ideological principles. Both extremes were detrimental (Greed 1994).

Colonial bankrolling. Many men active in the planning arena saw urban monumentality and advanced infrastructure as the physical representation of prosperity, culture, and civilisation (Flanagan 2018). But we cannot forget that the European and North American grand planning of the late nineteenth and early twentieth centuries was driven by the wealth extracted from colonial enterprises in Africa, Asia, and Latin America. The Second

Industrial Revolution is also known as the Age of Empire. (Even the Soviet Union, which officially took a strong anti-imperialist stance, exhibited many characteristics of an empire.) This economic backdrop is crucial to understanding the links between urban planning and the patriarchy.

Colonial powers benefited enormously from their dominions. Natural resources, agricultural products, and cheap labour flowed from the colonies to enrich the metropoles, placing them in an advantageous position to contemplate or embark on transformative urban plans and projects (Markus 2003). While the legacy of underground subways, broad boulevards, modern sewage systems, ornate museums, stately city halls, vast urban parks, and public housing for the working class may now be considered as positive, it is crucial to remember that it was underwritten by the exploitation and dispossession of colonised peoples.

Women's Different Planning Preoccupations

The educated or otherwise elite women who advocated for urban reform during the Second Industrial Revolution are generally considered "minor" planning figures (Hooper 1998). Their work – often without a spatial planning component – is seen as unglamorous compared with drawing grand plans, envisioning new types of transport infrastructure, and building imposing monuments (Spain 2001). However, women's contributions have been important and deserve mention here not least because their preoccupations were different from those of male planners, architects, and engineers. Women focused on housing policy and design, the needs of poor families, and children's upbringing in the industrial city. If this appears to suggest "gender essentialism," it is important to remember that gender roles were far more rigid during the Second Industrial Revolution, and women had limited access to architecture and planning education.

In England, a housing movement pioneer was Octavia Hill (1838–1912), a largely self-educated woman who entered the workforce in her early teens. As the owner and manager of many decayed inner-city properties that housed London's poor, she brought a humane touch to the landlord-tenant relationship (Meller 1995). By the late 1800s, Hill oversaw, with the help of other women she trained, more than 3,000 rental units. Rejecting the notion that only the innately immoral or inferior lived in dilapidated housing, she charged affordable rents and worked to renovate her properties, prioritising the welfare and stability of the residents. Instead of evicting tenants, she involved them in maintenance tasks and educated them to care for their own homes. She argued that urban renewal would follow as people's housing conditions improved (Hill 2019[1875]). Hill also campaigned to preserve green spaces and sought nearby indoor and outdoor spaces for children to study and play in (Crawford 1995). Beyond that, she was not interested in large-scale social engineering. Nor did she seek to restructure the metropolis to control the poor. An Ebenezer Howard contemporary, Hill lacked his religious tendencies and spurned his gender-based ideas of urban organisation (Hill 2019[1875]). Having lived among the working classes, she recognised that many women needed to work outside the home (Flanagan 2018).

While her approach and ideas were superior relative to contemporaneous housing management practices in English cities, Hill has been negatively portrayed in the literature as "the friendly face of landlordism," whose primary motive was to provide a return on investment to her financial backers (she applied the so-called 5 per cent philanthropy principle) (Clayton 2012; Frampton 1992). She has also been depicted as a bourgeois woman attempting to instil her own class values among poor tenants (Flanagan 2018).

Professional women made their presence known in the urban spaces of continental Europe too. In Berlin, for example, middle-class women's building societies and clubs, involving female architects and female patrons, began to appear around 1910. These served as venues for engagement with urban ills affecting women, such as poverty, disease, prostitution, and alcoholism. Of course, these issues were confronted in the male public sphere as well, but women's clubs approached them with more compassion and sensitivity to gender-based needs. A series of innovative ideas emerged from women's building societies. One was the collective residence for educated working women who did not choose the traditional path of marriage. Another was the retirement home for independent women who wished to avoid old-age homes run by religious and/or charitable organisations (Stratigakos 2001).

In the United States, feminist luminaries interested in urban reform included Melusina Fay Peirce (1836–1923), Marie Stevens Case Howland (1836–1921), Sarah Sophia Chase Platt-Decker (1856–1912), Charlotte Perkins Gilman (1860–1935), Alice Constance Austin (1862–1955), and Catherine Bauer (1905–1964). Some of them were part of the progressive Harvard Square Group in Massachusetts. Decker chaired the Federation of Associated Women's Clubs, and Austin was a self-taught architect. Bauer was an academic; she served as an adviser to various housing and planning agencies, and even chaired several of those agencies.

At various times these women sought to envision, design, promote, or even build experimental towns (or buildings) that were more responsive to gender-based needs. Sometimes their designs included radical feminist concepts such as houses without kitchens, cooperative housekeeping societies, and 24-hour childcare. The idea was to liberate women from domestic chores by centralising services such as laundry, cooking, baking, childcare, sewing, and cleaning (Greed 1994). Bauer was a leading public housing advocate.

The lives and careers of Peirce, Richards, Gilman, and Austin have been discussed at length by Hayden (1982). Spain (2001) has written about the work of Decker and other women involved in organisations such as the Young Women's Christian Association (YWCA) and the National Association of Colored Women (NACW). A biography of Bauer has been authored by Oberlander and Newbrun (1999). Here we only reiterate some key points from this literature.

Peirce's focus was on the domestic economy. She noted that the gendered division of labour during the Second Industrial Revolution forced middle-class women to perform inefficient, unpaid housework on an individual basis or led to the exploitation of poor women employed as cooks and maids. To free women from their domestic toil, Peirce introduced the concept of cooperative housekeeping, and even founded the short-lived Cambridge Cooperative Housekeeping Society in 1869. Married women participating in a cooperative housekeeping group would perform all their domestic work collectively – and thus more efficiently – and bill their husbands for it. Eventually, these changes would render obsolete the female-designated spaces of the house such as the kitchen and the laundry room. Based on this domestic program, Peirce envisioned a new residential neighbourhood design which contained rows of simple houses used for sleeping and socialising and larger facilities which centralised housekeeping tasks (Hayden 1981).

Like Peirce, Howland campaigned for cooperative housekeeping. But, as a believer in the economic independence of women, she proposed that the workplace (i.e. an ideal factory) rather than the residential neighbourhood be the focus of cooperative housekeeping activities. She expanded the notion of cooperative housekeeping to include nurseries, which would allow mothers to work, socialise, or even leave for a time. She popularised in the United States the concept of the Familistère,[2] which she had experienced first-hand in France. In addition, Howland helped create an experimental colony in Mexico in which she lived. Its aesthetics were basic but the plans contained innovations such as apartment hotels, kitchenless houses, and cooperative housekeeping facilities (Hayden 1981).

Decker was even more influential on the ground. While chairing the Federation of Associated Women's Clubs, she spearheaded the creation of "redemptive places" for poor migrants, including boarding houses, settlement houses, vocational schools, playgrounds, and public baths. Organisations such as the YWCA and NACW focused on helping women specifically, supporting their independence. Their small-sized, home-like environments, inspired by the religious doctrines and domestic ideologies of the era, helped newcomers adjust to the United States and meet their needs for healthcare, food, shelter, and childcare. The NACW addressed the needs of Black women in ways that the YWCA and other organisations did for white women. Decker's army of builders and team of female volunteers were active in cities ranging from Chicago to Washington, DC, long before formal government agencies were funded to deliver welfare services (Spain 2001).

In contrast to Peirce, Howland, and Decker, Gilman shunned the idea of cooperative or voluntary women's organisations. Instead, she endorsed the more economically conservative notion of large-scale domestic industry: commercial kitchens, laundries, and daycare centres. These facilities would support working mothers. As a humanitarian, Gilman believed in family and motherhood, in addition to urban efficiency and house minimalism. She further developed Howland's innovative concept of the 'feminist apartment hotel' with kitchenless private suites and centralised housework and childcare services, which would be performed by paid (female) professionals (Hayden 1981).

Austin's main legacy is a feminist Garden City which she designed and helped build in Southern California. Now in ruins, her city stood as a communitarian alternative to Los Angeles's hyper-capitalism. Austin proposed the idea of an urban infrastructure for cooked food delivery, dishwashing, and laundry services, aiming to free women from the oppressive traditional home (Figure 25). Public delivery systems and underground utilities would

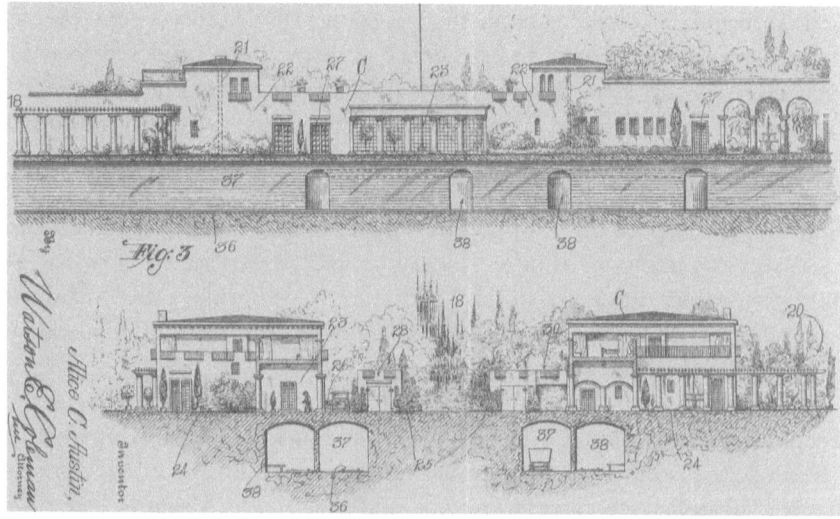

Figure 25 Austin's designs for kitchenless houses and meal delivery systems. Drawings from patent application. Source: Paul Kagan utopian communities collection, Beinecke Rare Book Library, Yale University. Image in the public domain.

support a restful, car-free city centre, with private automobiles used only for travel outside the city. Her design included concrete courtyard houses built in rows to foster community solidarity and ensure equal housing access. Each house had built-in furniture, rollaway beds, and tiled floors to reduce cleaning. Practically, this was the first comprehensive plan for a city without private housework (Hayden 1981). While her house designs were quite inventive, Austin's geometric urban layout with avenues radiating from a public centre reflected traditional utopian designs (Markus 2003).

Among her many contributions, Bauer introduced in the United States a series of housing concepts, policies, and designs she had researched in northern Europe. These included 'minimum standards' for all social classes, three-dimensional planning, tenant protections, and 'community units' which combined housing and auxiliary amenities (kindergartens, libraries, clinics, laundries, playgrounds, post offices, shops, restaurants, and the like). She believed that most of America's housing problems derived from market speculation. In her writings, she lamented that the ideal of home ownership, deeply rooted in the American frontier heritage, had been so heavily promoted that a significant portion of the population had come to view the housing market as "petty capitalists" rather than as workers and consumers. To Bauer, the solution to urban housing problems such as disrepair and unaffordability was not a return to semi-rural living, as proposed by Howard, Geddes, and other male urban reformers, or mill towns like Saltaire and Pullman, which she called a nineteenth-century "abomination." She was in favour of municipal purchases of land for non-profit housing use (Bauer 2021[1934]).

Considered together, these female reformers – by no means infallible – were more acute observers of people's lived experience in the city than male planners, architects, and engineers, who more often dealt in abstract theorising. In other words, women worried about the human condition while men's focus was on built structures and infrastructure. Rather than stretching or clearing out the existing city fabric, women sought to restore it. Practically, they extended their reproductive duties within the home to the entire urban space (Flanagan 2018). This aligns with the ideals of a social-anarcha-feminist city, where all members of society, including planners, are expected to act as 'good mothers' – bearing responsibility for one another's daily welfare and caring for others equally (see Goettner-Abendroth 2010).

CONCLUSION

In the twenty-first century, after so many failed experiments, has the concept of 'urban utopia' finally become obsolete? Certainly not. Futuristic cities and communities are still being envisioned. Dulik (2023) lists several North American examples proposed or backed by major private corporations or individual male billionaires: Donald Trump's "Freedom Cities" to be built on federal land; Elon Musk's Snailbrook, a private "Texas utopia" for his employees; Praxis Society's "city-cryptostate" in the Mediterranean, supported by major Silicon Valley venture capitalists including Peter Thiel and the Winklevoss twins; Marc Lore's "Telosa" in the American Southwest or Appalachia; Alphabet's "smart" neighbourhood in Toronto; and Meta's Willow Village next to its headquarters in Northern California. These models are as patriarchal as the ones we critiqued in this book. Moreover, many amount to conservative techno-utopias, lacking the social progressivism of some of the early models we discussed.

Sadly, outlandish visions are no longer confined to the North Atlantic. As the world goes through a Fourth Industrial Revolution, and wealth grows everywhere alongside inequality, masculinist dystopias are being proposed or built across Asia, Africa, and Latin America. While outwardly glossy, projects like Masdar City in the United Arab Emirates, NEOM in Saudi Arabia, Próspera in Honduras, Bitcoin City in El Salvador, and Zim Cyber City in Zimbabwe "serve as little more than geopolitical PR projects, intended to launder reputations and absorb international investment" into "deregulated crypto-ruled tax havens" (Dulik 2023). This is disquieting, more so because, given the financial and political clout of their patrons, the realisation of these proposals appears to be inevitable.

However, progressive planners and the communities they serve have a moral duty to shake the torpor induced by the status quo and use their imagination to uproot neoliberal patriarchy from urban planning.[1] Together they can translate feminist planning principles into spatial forms. Perhaps a co-design approach is, in itself, utopian. But all feminist thinking – whether in literature, economics, or planning – is inherently utopian as a gender-equal or gender-free society has never existed in history (Mellor 1982). While perfection may not be attainable, the pursuit of a utopian ideal remains worthwhile as long as it encourages critical reflection on current systems, pushing people to question inequalities and unsustainable practices, while exploring alternative models of living, governance, and community. At the very least, it offers hope for a city that is more just, prosperous, healthy, green, and beautiful.

REFERENCES

Abercrombie, P., Childs, D.R. 1959[1933]. *Town and Country Planning* (3rd ed.) London: Oxford University Press.
Aibar, E., Bijker, W. 1997. Constructing a city: The Cerdà plan for the extension of Barcelona. *Science, Technology, & Human Values* 22(1): 3–30.
Akcan, E. 2006. Toward a cosmopolitan ethics in architecture: Bruno Taut's translations out of Germany. *New German Critique* 99: 7–39.
Alphand, A. 1867. *Les Promenades de Paris*. Paris: J. Rothschild.
Amati, M., Freestone, R. 2009. 'Saint Patrick': Sir Patrick Abercrombie's Australian tour 1948. *The Town Planning Review* 80(6): 597–626.
Ashworth, W. 1954. *The Genesis of Modern British Town Planning*. London: Routledge.
Baar, K. 1992. The national movement to halt the spread of multifamily housing, 1890–1926. *Journal of the American Planning Association* 58(1): 39–48.
Balgarnie, R. 1878. *Sir Titus Salt, Baronet: His Life and its Lessons*. London: Hodder and Stoughton.
Barr, M., Smith, N. 1983. *Women and Utopia: Critical Interpretations*. Lanham, NY: University Press of America.
Bartkowski, F. 1989. *Feminist Utopias*. Lincoln, Nb: University of Nebraska Press.
Bassam, N. 2023. *The Gendered City: How Cities Keep Failing Women*. Milan: Self-published.
Bauer, C., 2021[1934]. Elements of modern housing. In R. LeGates, F. Stout (eds), *Early Urban Planning VI*, pp. 1–237. London: Routledge.
Baumeister, R. 1876. *Stadt-Erweiterungen in technischer, baupolizeilicher und wirthschaftlicher Beziehung* [Town Extensions: Their Links with Technical and Economic Concerns and with Building Regulations]. Germany: Ernst & Korn.
Baxter, J.E. 2012. The paradox of a capitalist utopia: Visionary ideals and lived experience in the Pullman community 1880–1900. *International Journal of Historical Archaeology* 16(4): 651–665.
Beck, J. 2009. John Nolen and his political ordering of landscapes. PhD thesis, University of Pennsylvania, Philadelphia, PA.
Bellamy, E. 1967 [1888]. *Looking Backward: 2000–1887*. Cambridge: Harvard University Press.
Bersky, A. 2013. Le Corbusier and the sexism of architecture. *Architect Magazine*, 20 August.
Bingaman, A., Sanders, L., Zorach, R. 2002. *Embodied Utopias: Gender, Social Change and the Modern Metropolis*. London: Routledge.
Birolli, V. 2016. Antonio Sant'Elia et La Città Nuova: Représenter la ville moderne. *Livraisons de l'Histoire de l'Architecture* 32: 89–104.

Boileau, I. 1959. La Ciudad Lineal: A critical study of the linear suburb of Madrid. *The Town Planning Review* 30(3): 230–238.

Borderías, C., López-Guallar, P. 2001. La Teoría del Salario Obrero y la Subestimación del Trabajo Femenino en Ildefons Cerdà [Theory of Workers' Salary and the Underestimation of Women's Work in Ildefons Cerdà]. Barcelona: Arxiu Històric de la Ciutat.

Bosman, C., Grant-Smith, D., Osborne, N. 2017. Women in planning in the twenty-first century. *Australian Planner* 54(1): 1–5.

Bottici, C. 2022. *Anarchafeminism*. New York: Bloomsbury.

Buder, S. 1966. Pullman: An experiment in industrial order and community planning, 1880–1930. PhD thesis, University of Chicago, Chicago.

Budzynski, S. 2016. The spatialization of avant-garde consciousness: Antonio Sant'Elia's Città Nuova and the experience of modernity in Italy. In M. Branland (ed.), *1914: Guerre et Avant-Gardes*, pp. 39–46. Nanterre: Paris Ouest University Press.

Bullock, N. 1988. First the kitchen: Then the façade. *Journal of Design History* 1(3/4): 177–192.

Buls, C. 1893. *L'Esthétique des villes* [Urban Aesthetics]. 2. éd. Bruxelles: Bruyland-Christophe.

Burnham, D., Bennett, E. 1909. Plan of Chicago, prepared under the direction of the Commercial Club during the years MCMVI, MCMVII, and MCMVIII. Report, edited by C. Moore (ed.), Chicago.

Caramel, L., Longatti, A. 1988. *Antonio Sant'Elia: The Complete Works*. New York: Rizzoli.

Carmona, M. 2002. *Haussmann: His Life and Times, and the Making of Modern Paris*. Translated from the French by P. Camiller. Chicago: Ivan R. Dee.

Carranza, L. 1994. Le Corbusier and the problems of representation. *Journal of Architectural Education* 48(2): 70–81.

Cerdà, I. 2017[1867]. *General Theory of Urbanization*. Barcelona: Institute for Advanced Architecture of Catalonia.

Cherry, G. 1979. The town planning movement and the late Victorian city. *Transactions of the Institute of British Geographers* 4(2): 306–319.

City of New York, Board of Estimate and Apportionment. 1916. *Building Zone Resolution*.

Clark, B., Howard, E. 2003. Ebenezer Howard and the marriage of town and country: An introduction to Howard's Garden Cities of To-morrow. Excerpts from Garden Cities of To-Morrow. *Organization & Environment* 16(1): 87–97.

Clayton, P. 2012. *Octavia Hill: Social Reformer and Co-founder of the National Trust*. London: Pitkin.

Cliff, T., Harman, C. 1974. *State Capitalism in Russia*. London: Pluto Press.

Coleman, A., Brown, S., Cottle, L., Marshall, P., Redknap, C., Sex, R. 1985. *Utopia on Trial: Vision and Reality in Planned Housing*. London: Hilary Shipman.

Colistra, D. 2023. The City Crown, or the 'social sublime'. *Diségno* 12: 227–232.

Collins, G. 1959a. Linear planning throughout the world. *Journal of the Society of Architectural Historians* 18(3): 74–93.

Collins, G. 1959b. The Ciudad Lineal of Madrid. *Journal of the Society of Architectural Historians* 18(2): 38–53.

Collins, G. 1974. Preface to *Sotsgorod: The Problem of Building Socialist Cities*. Cambridge, MA: The MIT Press.

Collins, G., Collins, C.C. 1965. *Camillo Sitte and the Birth of Modern Planning*. New York: Random House.

Cortjaens, W. 2011. "The German way of making better cities": German reconstruction plans for Belgium during the First World War. In L. Verpoest, N. Bullock (eds), *Living* with History, 1914–1964: Rebuilding Europe after the First and Second World Wars and the Role of Heritage Preservation, pp. 44–59. Leuven: Leuven University Press.

Cranz, G. 1980. Women in urban parks. *Signs: Journal of Women in Culture and Society* 5(S3): S79–S95.

Crawford, M. 1995. *Building the Workingman's Paradise*. New York: Verso.

Creese, W. 1994. An extended planning progression from the late nineteenth to early twentieth century. In R. Unwin (ed.), *Town Planning in Practice: An Introduction to the Art of Designing Cities and Suburb*, pp. vii–xxv. Princeton, NJ: Princeton Architectural Press.

Dehaene, M. 2004. Urban lessons for the modern planner: Patrick Abercrombie and the study of urban development. *The Town Planning Review* 75(1): 1–30.

Dewhirst, R.K. 1960. Saltaire. *The Town Planning Review* 31(2): 135–144.

Dishman, A. 2020. Seeking the 'hidden histories' of the Victorian child-millworker as offspring, worker and pupil in Saltaire, West Yorkshire, 1853–1878. Ed thesis, University of Sheffield, Sheffield.

Dougherty, J. 1981. Broadacre City: Frank Lloyd Wrights utopia. *The Centennial Review* 25(3): 239–256.

Doxiadis, C.A. 1967. On linear cities. *The Town Planning Review* 38(1): 35–42.

Dulik, C. 2023. Impossible cities: The billionaire's urban fantasia. *The Baffler* 68, May.

East, M. 2024. *What if Women Designed the City? 33 Leverage Points to Make Your City Work Better for Women and Girls*. Dorset: Triarchy Press.

Eaton, R. 2002. *Ideal Cities: Utopianism and the (Un)Built Environment*. London: Thames & Hudson.

Elkin, L. 2017. *Flâneuse: Women Walk the City in Paris, New York, Tokyo, Venice, and London*. New York: Farrar, Straus and Giroux.

Fainstein, S.S., Servon, L.J. (eds.) 2005. *Gender and Planning: A Reader*. New Brunswick, NJ: Rutgers University Press.

Fishman, R. 1982. *Urban Utopias in the Twentieth Century: Ebenezer Howard, Frank Lloyd Wright, and Le Corbusier*. Boston: MIT Press.

Flanagan, M. 2013. The city, still the hope of democracy? From Jane Addams and Mary Parker Follett to the Arab Spring. *The Journal of the Gilded Age and Progressive Era* 12(1): 5–29.

Flanagan, M. 2018. *Constructing the Patriarchal City: Gender and the Built Environments of London, Dublin, Toronto, and Chicago, 1870s into the 1940s*. Philadelphia: Temple University Press.

Frampton, K. 1992. Tony Garnier and the industrial city 1899–1918. In *Modern Architecture: A Critical History*, pp. 100–104. New York: Thames & Hudson.

Fraser, B. 2019. Obsessively writing the modern city: The partial madness of urban planning culture and the case of Arturo Soria y Mata in Madrid, Spain. *Journal of Literary & Cultural Disability Studies* 13(1): 21–37.

Freemark, Y., Bliss, A., Vale, L. 2022. Housing Haussmann's Paris: The politics and legacy of Second Empire redevelopment. *Planning Perspectives* 37(2): 293–317.

Frisby, D. 1997. The metropolis as text: Otto Wagner and Vienna's second renaissance. *Culture, Theory and Critique* 40(1): 1–16.

Frisby, D. 2003. Straight or crooked streets? The contested rational spirit of the modern metropolis. In I.B. Whyte (ed.), *Modernism and the Spirit of the City*, pp. 57–84. London: Routledge.

Garnier, T. 1989[1917]. *Une Cité Industrielle: Étude pour la Construction des Villes*. New York: Princeton Architectural Press.

Geddes, P. 1949. *Cities in Evolution*. London: Williams & Norgate.

Geretsegger, H., Peintner, M. 1970. *Otto Wagner 1841–1918: The Expanding City, the Beginning of Modern Architecture.* London: Pall Mall Press.
Ghodsee, K.R. 2023. *Everyday Utopia: What 2,000 Years of Wild Experiments can Teach us about the Good Life.* New York: Simon & Schuster.
Goettner-Abendroth, H. 2010. Matriarchy. In A. O'Reilly (ed.), *Encyclopedia of Motherhood*, pp. 732–734. Thousand Oaks, CA: Sage.
González, E.R., Irazábal, C. 2015. Emerging issues in planning: Ethno-racial intersections. *Local Environment* 20(6): 600–610.
Greed, C. 1994. *Women and Planning: Creating Gendered Realities.* London: Routledge.
Hall, P. 1995. Bringing Abercrombie Back from the shades: A look forward and back. *The Town Planning Review* 66(3): 227–241.
Hanisch, R. 2010. Camillo Sitte: City planning according to artistic principles, Vienna 1889. In C.H. Cordua *Manifestoes and Transformations in the Early Modernist City*, pp. 125–135. London: Taylor & Francis.
Hardy, D. 2012. *Utopian England: Community Experiments 1900–1945.* London: Routledge.
Hayden, D. 1976. *Seven American Utopias: The Architecture of Communitarian Socialism, 1790–1975.* Boston, MA: MIT Press.
Hayden, D. 1982. *The Grand Domestic Revolution: A History of Feminist Designs for American Homes, Neighborhoods, and Cities.* Boston: MIT Press.
Hayden, D. 2004. *Building Suburbia: Green Fields and Urban Growth, 1820–2000.* New York: Vintage.
Hein, C. 2010. Shaping Tokyo: Land development and planning practice in the early modern Japanese metropolis. *Journal of Urban History* 36(4): 447–484.
Hendler, S. 2005. Towards a feminist code of planning ethics. *Planning Theory & Practice* 6(1): 53–69.
Hermansen-Cordua, C. 2010. The idea of modernity in Cerdà's Teoría General de la Urbanización. In C. Hermansen-Cordua (ed.), *Manifestoes and Transformations in the Early Modernist City*, pp. 79–104. London: Routledge.
Hill, O. 2019[1875]. *Homes of the London Poor.* Project Gutenberg. New York: State Charities Aid Association.
Holroyd, A. 1871. *Saltaire, and its Founder, Sir Titus Salt, Bart, Making of the Modern World* (2nd ed.). Saltaire: Abraham Holroyd.
Hooper, B. 1998. The poem of male desires: female bodies, modernity, and "Paris, capital of the nineteenth century". In L. Sandercock (ed.), *Making the Invisible Visible: A Multicultural Planning History*, pp. 227–255. Berkeley, CA: University of California Press.
Hooper, B. 2002. Urban space, modernity, and masculinist desire: the utopian longings of Le Corbusier. In Bingman, A., Sanders, L., Zorach, R. (eds), *Embodied Utopias: Gender, Social Change, and the Modern Metropolis*, pp. 55–78. London: Routledge.
Hoover, D.P. 1988. Women in nineteenth-century Pullman. Master's thesis, University of Arizona, Tucson, Az.
Howard, E. 1902. *Garden Cities of Tomorrow.* London: Swan Sonnenschein & Co.
Jacobs, J. 1961. *The Death and Life of Great American Cities.* New York: Vintage.
Jensen, L. 2004. The photographs of Jacob Riis: History in relation to truth. *Constructing the Past* 5(1): 6.
Johns, A. 2010. Feminism and utopianism. In G. Claeys (ed.), *The Cambridge Companion to Utopian Literature*, pp. 174–199. Cambridge: Cambridge University Press.

REFERENCES

Johnson, P. 2015. Feminism and humanism. In A. Copson, A.C. Grayling (eds), *The Wiley Blackwell Handbook of Humanism*, chapter 16. New York: Wiley.

Jordan, D.P. 1992. The city: Baron Haussmann and modern Paris. *The American Scholar* 61(1): 99–106.

Jordan, D.P. 1995. *Transforming Paris: The Life and Labors of Baron Haussman*. New York: Simon & Schuster.

Kalms, N. 2024. *She City: Designing Out Women's Inequity in Cities*. New York: Bloomsbury.

Kern, L. 2020. *Feminist City: Claiming Space in a Man-made World*. New York: Verso Books.

Kessler, C.F. 1984. *Daring to Dream: Utopian Stories by United States Women, 1836–1919*. Boston, MA: Pandora Press.

Kessler, M. 2005. Filters and pathologies: Caillebotte and Manet in Haussmann's Paris. *Nineteenth-Century Contexts* 27(3): 245–268.

Ladd, B. 1987. Urban aesthetics and the discovery of the urban fabric in turn-of-the-century Germany. *Planning Perspectives* 2(3): 270–286.

Le Corbusier. 1964[1933]. *The Radiant City: Elements of a Doctrine of Urbanism to be Used as the Basis of our Machine-Age Civilization*. London: Orion Press.

Lindsey, A. 1939. Paternalism and the Pullman strike. *The American Historical Review* 44(2): 272–289.

Lynch, Tim. 2006. Saltaire: The Town That Titus Built. (Titus Salt's City for Economic Development). *British Heritage* 27(3): 50–52.

Marcus, S. 2001. Haussmannization as anti-modernity: The Apartment house in Parisian urban discourse, 1850–1880. *Journal of Urban History* 27(6): 723–745.

Markus, T.A. 2003. Is there a built form for non-patriarchal utopias? In A. Bingaman, L. Sanders, R. Zorach (eds), *Embodied Utopias*, pp. 15–32. London: Routledge.

Martín-Ramos, A. 2012. The Cerdà effect on city modernisation. *The Town Planning Review* 83(6): 695–716.

Mehan, A. 2017. The empty locus of power: Production of political urbanism in modern Tehran. PhD thesis, Polytechnic University of Turin, Turin.

Meller, H. 1990. Planning theory and women's role in the city. *Urban History Yearbook* 17: 85–98.

Meller, H. 1995. Urban renewal and citizenship: The quality of life in British cities, 1890–1990. *Urban History* 22 (1): 63–84.

Meller, H. 2004. Women and citizenship: Gender and the built environment in British cities, 1870–1939. In D. Reeder, R. Rodger, R. Colls (eds), *Cities of Ideas: Civil Society and Urban Governance in Britain 1800–2000*, pp. 234–239. Burlington, Vt: Ashgate.

Mellor, A. 1982. On feminist utopias. *Women's Studies* 9(3): 241–262.

Mies, M., Shiva, V. 2014. *Ecofeminism* (2nd ed.) London: Zed Books.

Miliutin, N. 2021[1930]. *Sotsgorod: The Problem of Building Socialist Cities*. Translated from the Russian by Arthur Sprague. Cambridge, MA: MIT Press.

Miller, T. 2017. Expressionist utopia: Bruno Taut, glass architecture, and the dissolution of cities. *Filozofski Vestnik* 38(1): 107–129.

Moravánszky, Á. 2006. Camillo Sitte: Romantic or realist? The picturesque city reconsidered. *East Central Europe* 33(1–2): 293–308.

Mozingo, L.A., Jewell, L. 2011. *Women in Landscape Architecture*. Jefferson, NC: McFarland & Company.

Mumford, L. 1922. *The Story of Utopias*. New York: Boni & Liveright.

Neuman, M. 2011. Ildefons Cerdà and the future of spatial planning: The network urbanism of a city planning pioneer. *The Town Planning Review* 82(2): 117–143.

Nolen, J. 2014[1919]. *New Ideals in the Planning of Cities, Towns and Villages*. London: Routledge.
Noyes, J.H. 2019[1870]. *History of American Socialisms*. Glasgow: Good Press.
Oberlander, P., Newbrun, E. 1999. *Houser: The Life and Work of Catherine Bauer*. Vancouver, B.C.: University of British Columbia Press.
Olmstead, F.L. 1922. *Frederick Law Olmstead: Early Years and Experiences*. New York: G.P. Putnam's Sons.
Pearson, C. 1977. Women's fantasies and feminist utopias. *Frontiers: A Journal of Women Studies* 2(3): 50–61.
Pojani, D. 2021. *Trophy Cities: A Feminist Perspective on New Capitals*. London: Edward Elgar.
Pojani, D., Sagaris, L., Papa, E. 2021. Editorial of special issue on 'transport, gender, culture'. *Transportation Research Part A: Policy and Practice* 144: 34–36.
Pojani, D., Wardale, D., Brown, K. 2018. Sexism and the city: how urban planning has failed women. *The Conversation*, 17 April.
Pullman Company, 2020. Labor and race relations: Pullman and the African-American experience. *Pullman Museum*, available at: www.pullman-museum.org/labor, last accessed on 28 February 2024.
Reiff, J.L. 1997. A modern Lear and his daughters: Gender in the model town of Pullman. *Journal of Urban History* 23(3): 316–341.
Reiff, J.L., Hirsch, S.E. 1989. Pullman and its public: Image and aim in making and interpreting history. *The Public Historian* 11(4): 99–112.
Riis, J. 1890. *How the Other Half Lives: Studies among the Tenements of New York*. New York: Charles Scribner's Sons.
Robinson, C. M. 1901. *The Improvement of Towns and Cities, or, The Practical Basis of Civic Aesthetics*. New York: Putnam.
Rosenau, H. 1959. *The Ideal City in its Architectural Evolution*. London: Routledge.
Samuel, F. 2004. *Le Corbusier: Architect and Feminist*. Hoboken, NJ: Wiley.
Sánchez de Madariaga, I.S., Neuman, M. (eds.) 2020. *Engendering Cities: Designing Sustainable Urban Spaces for All*. London: Routledge.
Scheper, G.L. 1989. The reformist vision of Frederick Law Olmsted and the poetics of park design. *The New England Quarterly* 62(3): 369–402.
Schorske, C. 1981. *Fin-de-Siècle Vienna: Politics and Culture*. Cambridge: Cambridge University Press.
Sewell, J.E., 2022. Women: Complex lives in the patriarchal city. In D. Pojani (ed.), *Alternative Planning History and Theory*, pp. 15–30. London: Routledge.
Sitte, C. 1945[1889]. *The Art of Building Cities*. Translated from the German by C. Steward. New York: Reinhold.
Smith, C. 2006. *The Plan of Chicago* (1st ed.). Chicago: University of Chicago Press.
Sonne, W. 2009. Political connotations of the picturesque. In C. Bohl, J.F. Lejeune (eds), *Sitte, Hegemann and the Metropolis*, pp. 143–160. London: Routledge.
Soria y Mata, A. 1892[2004]. *The Linear City*. Translated from the Spanish by M. Diaz Gonzales. In R. LeGates, F. Stout (eds), F. *Early Urban Planning VI*, pp. 1–25. London: Routledge.
Soria y Puig, A. 1995. Ildefonso Cerdà's General Theory of 'Urbanización'. *The Town Planning Review* 66(1): 15–39.
Spain, D. 2001. *How Women Saved the City*. Minneapolis/St Paul: University of Minnesota Press.
Staples, B. 2019. The death of the Black utopia. *The New York Times*, 28 November.

Starostenko, J. 2019. The J. Stübben's book "Der Städtebau" ("Town Planning") and its influence on the works of Russian specialists in cities improvement of the early 20th century. *Advances in Social Science, Education and Humanities Research* 34: 438–441.

Stephenson, R.B. 2015a. *John Nolen, Landscape Architect and City Planner*. Amherst, MA.: University of Massachusetts Press.

Stephenson, R.B. 2015b. John Nolan: Racism and city planning. *View* 15: 8–11.

Stratigakos, D. 2016. *Where Are the Women Architects?* Princeton, NJ: Princeton University Press.

Stratigakos, D. 2001. A women's Berlin: How female patrons and architects in imperial Germany re-gendered the city. In A. Bingaman, L. Sanders, R. Zorach (eds), *Embodied Utopias*, pp. 139–155. London: Routledge.

Stübben, J. 2008[1907]. *Urban Planning*. Translated from the German by A. Albrecht. Foreword by Julia Koschinsky and Emily Talen. Chicago: University of Chicago Press.

Taut, B. 2009[1919]. The City Crown. Translated by U. Altenmüller and M. Mindrup. *Journal of Architectural Education* 63(1): 120–134.

Unwin, R. 1994[1909]. *Town Planning in Practice: An Introduction to the Art of Designing Cities and Suburbs*. Princeton, NJ: Princeton Architectural Press.

Vujosevic, T. 2017. *Modernism and the Making of the Soviet New Man*. Manchester: Manchester University Press.

Wagner, O. 1912. The development of a great city. *The Architectural Record* 31(5): 485–500.

Wacker, C. H. 1911. *Wacker's Manual of the Plan of Chicago: Municipal Economy*. Chicago: The Chicago Plan Commission.

Watson, J. 2019. The suburbanity of Frank Lloyd Wright's Broadacre City. *Journal of Urban History* 45(5): 1010–1029.

Weeks, W. 1999. *The Man who Made Paris Paris: The Illustrated Biography of Georges-Eugène Haussmann*. London: Allison & Busby.

White, J. 2019. The 'dismemberment of London': Chamberlain, Abercrombie and the London Plans of 1943–44. *The London Journal* 44(3): 206–26.

Whyte, I.B. 1982. *Bruno Taut and the Architecture of Activism*. Cambridge: Cambridge University Press.

Wiebenson, D. 1960. Utopian aspects of Tony Garnier's Cité Industrielle. *Journal of the Society of Architectural Historians* 19(1): 16–24.

Willsher, K. 2016. Story of cities #12: Haussmann rips up Paris. *The Guardian*, 31 March.

Wilson, E. 1992. *The Sphinx in the City: Urban Life, the Control of Disorder, and Women*. Berkeley, CA: University of California Press.

Wright, F.L. 1932. *The Disappearing City*. New York: W. F. Payson.

Wynn, M. 1979. Barcelona: Planning and change. *The Town Planning Review* 50(2): 185–203.

NOTES

Introduction

1. See, for example, Bosman et al. (2017) for discussions of women in planning; González and Irazábal (2015) for an intersectional lens; and Pojani et al. (2021) for a focus on mobility.
2. The First Industrial Revolution (circa 1750–1850) marked the transition from agrarian economies to industrialised ones, with innovations such as the steam engine and mechanised textile production transforming manufacturing. The Second Industrial Revolution (circa 1850–interwar) saw rapid industrialisation fuelled by advances in steel production, electricity, and mass production techniques, leading to large-scale urbanisation. The Third Industrial Revolution (post–World War II–2000s) was driven by the rise of computers, IT, and automation. The Fourth Industrial Revolution, currently underway, is characterised by artificial intelligence (AI), the Internet of Things (IoT), and robotics.
3. Many argue that the North Atlantic is now in a post-industrial phase, where the focus has shifted from industrial manufacturing to services, technology, and information sectors. However, many foundational elements of industrial capitalism, like private ownership and profit motives, continue to influence the economy.
4. For example, in New York, pioneering photojournalism by Jacob Riis exposed the squalid conditions of impoverished tenements, shocking the city's middle and upper classes (Riis 1890). Riis showed sympathy for his photography subjects, particularly women and children, and attributed their plight to poor environmental conditions. However, he was also judgemental of the "undeserving poor" – i.e. those he saw as lazy, criminal, or prone to vice. A Danish émigré himself, he wrote with prejudice about other migrant groups (Jews, Italians, and Irishmen). It later emerged that some of his photographs were staged (Jensen 2004).
5. In this overview, we refer to books that primarily cover utopian cities and settlements conceived in the West in the nineteenth century and after. A number of authors have discussed the physical manifestations of utopias in Classical Antiquity, the Renaissance, the Enlightenment, as well as in East and South Asia (i.e. regions where Buddhism is widespread), but those eras and locations are beyond the scope of this book. We have also excluded books that discuss utopias from a literary, philosophical, technological, political, religious, or artistic perspective, without delving into architecture or urban design. An exception is made for books on *feminist* utopias.
6. Material feminism is a theoretical framework that emphasises the ways in which economic structures (i.e. material conditions) shape gender inequality.

7. There is also a considerable body of literature which elaborates on the trope of the trapped suburban housewife (Greed, 1994), while falling short of envisioning a utopian alternative for women.
8. Charles Fourier (1772–1837) was a French social reformer. Fourier's utopian settlements were envisioned as a single building called a Phalanstère (or 'grand hotel' modelled after Versailles). This housed a communal farming unit (a phalanxe or phalange) dedicated to the well-being of its members, where roles were constantly rotated among individuals.
9. Robert Owen (1771–1858) was a Welsh industrialist, philanthropist, and social reformer. He was a key figure in utopian socialism and the cooperative movement. A contemporary of Charles Fourier, he envisioned small, low-density utopian communities all living in one building equipped with sleeping quarters and public facilities.
10. We wished to consult the writings of the planners covered in this book, in addition to perusing secondary sources.
11. German engineer and academic, who is generally credited with having laid the foundation for planning as a scientific discipline. Baumeister was a pioneer of the zoning concept. His main book, *Stadterweiterungen in technischer, baupolizeilicher und Wirtschaftlicher Beziehung* [Town Extensions: Their Links with Technical and Economic Concerns and with Building Regulations] (1876), is only available in German. Just one portion (a chapter on sewer systems) has been translated into English.
12. Belgian politician and planning amateur, who served as mayor of Brussels in the late nineteenth century. An abridged version of his short essay *L'Esthétique des villes* [Urban Aesthetics] (1893) which supported Camillo Sitte's position, was translated into English and appeared in an issue of *Municipal Affairs* (1899) devoted to the City Beautiful. Other than this translation, very little material is available in English about Bul. A book with the same title appeared in 1908, which was written by a lesser-known French author, Emile Magne.
13. Dutch architect, renowned for the design of individual buildings (e.g. the Stock Exchange in Amsterdam) as well as the layout of several neighbourhoods in cities throughout The Netherlands.
14. French urban planner, credited with the invention of the roundabout (*carrefour à girations*) and the stepped boulevard design (*boulevard à redans*).
15. As noted earlier, Mumford was a renowned planning theorist and historian who extensively explored the relationship between human societies and their urban environments. His most influential planning book, *The City in History*, was not written until 1961.
16. Moses was a powerful public official who significantly reshaped New York City through his ambitious infrastructure projects, including highways and bridges. His tenure was marked by both transformative urban development and controversial decisions that displaced local communities and ignored public opposition.
17. Best known for writing Wacker's Manual (1911), a text commissioned by the Chicago Plan Commission to promote adoption of Daniel Burnham's 1909 Plan of Chicago (see page 50).
18. A lawyer, politician, and social reformer.
19. A lawyer and politician, he is considered 'the father of American zoning', having written the first comprehensive zoning ordinance (for New York City, 1916).
20. An economist and academic involved in Franklin Roosevelt's New Deal.

21. An architect educated in the United States and France, Ford was interested in technical building aspects such as height, bulk, and form, and believed in planning as a scientific discipline. He was also involved in the preparation of several regional plans for American cities.
22. For more authors, see the American Planning Association's list of essential books from every decade starting in 1909: www.planning.org/library/greatbooks.
23. Richardson wrote a non-fiction book, *Hygeia, a City of Health*, in 1876. He envisioned a utopian city designed with advanced public health principles to promote the well-being and longevity of its inhabitants.
24. Bellamy's novel *Looking Backward, 2000 to 1887* (1888) imagines a future utopian society in the year 2000, where socio-economic inequalities have been eradicated through a system of cooperative ownership and shared wealth. Women have equal opportunities and are freed from traditional domestic constraints.
25. A journalist, academic, and urban beautification advocate. Robinson's main book is *The Improvement of Towns and Cities, or, the Practical Basis of Civic Aesthetics* (1901).
26. A civil engineer practising in New York, he wrote *The Planning of the Modern City: A Review of the Principles Governing City Planning* in 1916.
27. Originally from Germany but spent his formative years in the United States Hegemann became one of the main agents of the transfer of American modernity and pragmatism to Europe. His major theoretical work was *The American Vitruvius; An Architect's Handbook of Civic Art* (1922), co-authored with Elbert Peets.
28. An exhibit at the 1939 New York World's Fair, Futurama was characterised by automated highways and vast suburbs. It was envisioned by Norman Bel Geddes, a stage and industrial designer.

Analysis

1. A "stroad" is a neologism describing a hybrid of a street and a road, which typically fails to function well as either.
2. He later moved towards functionalism.
3. Before *Sotsgorod*, Russian books about city planning – by Dubelier, Semenov, Ensh, and Dikansky – were more technical than revolutionary. Their main inspiration came from practical authors such as Josef Stübben (Starostenko 2019).
4. Known as 'Pullman cars'.
5. In the Spain of that era, engineers were regarded as progressive by virtue of their association with the emerging industrial class, whereas architects were seen as representing the old aristocracy.
6. The book was designed to span four volumes. Only the first two volumes were released; these were rather dry and technical and did not hold broad appeal. Volume 1 consists of a lengthy history and theory of planning, while Volume 2 is entirely made up of statistics. The third and fourth volumes, focusing on practical applications of theory and the specific case of Barcelona, were either left unpublished or never discovered.
7. In recent years, Barcelona has introduced the superblocks concept (*superilles* in Catalan) to reduce car dominance in the city. The superblock model reorganises urban space by grouping multiple city blocks (usually nine) into one larger block, where through-traffic is restricted and streets within the superblock are prioritised for pedestrians, cyclists, and local residents.

8. From 1881 to 1898, he was the chief municipal planner of Cologne.
9. The development of Vienna's ring road after the demolition of the old city walls.
10. He worked in partnership with Barry Parker, another English architect and planner associated with the Arts and Crafts movement.

Synthesis

1. Short for 'traditional wife'. The term 'trad wife' has gained attention in recent years, especially online, as part of broader cultural discussions about gender roles and feminism.
2. A version of Fourier's Phalanstère, developed by Jean-Baptiste André Godin, one of Fourier's leading disciples in Europe.

Conclusion

1. At the start of this book, we talked about 'industrial capitalism' as a force shaping planning during our timeline. Contemporary neoliberalism differs from industrial capitalism in its emphasis on deregulation, financial markets, privatisation, capital mobility, consolidation, and globalisation, compared to the earlier focus on manufacturing, minimal labour rights, and significant government-supported infrastructure development.

www.ingramcontent.com/pod-product-compliance
Lightning Source LLC
Chambersburg PA
CBHW030143170426
43199CB00008B/179